The
Joy of
Praying
the
Rosary

James

Resurrection Press
An Imprint of
CATHOLIC BOOK PUBLISHING CO.
Totowa • New Jersey

All proceeds from this book will go to *Christa House: The Jerry Hartman Residence*, a home for the dying poor on the grounds of Our Lady of Grace Church in West Babylon, New York.

— · — · — · —

Grateful acknowledgement is made to to *The Long Island Catholic* to reproduce essays contained in these pages.

— · — · — · —

Scripture quotations are from THE JERUSALEM BIBLE, copyright © 1966 by Darton, Longman & Todd, Ltd. and Doubleday, a division of Bantam, Doubleday, Dell Publishing Group, Inc. Reprinted by permission.

First published in October, 2003 by Resurrection Press, Catholic Book Publishing Company.

Copyright © 2003 by James M. McNamarra

ISBN 1-878718-87-8

Library of Congress Catalog Number: 2003111486

Cover design by Beth DeNapoli

Printed in the United States of America.

1 2 3 4 5 6 7 8 9

DEDICATION

To my sister Mary E. Mannkopf

In life she taught me to laugh.

When she was dying she asked me how to die. I ventured the statement that she should ask Jesus to bring her to Him. In a whispered voice she asked: "Can I add something to that? Can I say hurry up?" I said: "Yes, you can say: 'Hurry up. Hurry up is a prayer.'"

May she enjoy the peace God has given her.

Acknowledgements

I am grateful to the Sisters of the Atonement at St. Anthony's Guesthouse in Assisi for their hospitality and friendship when I stayed with them while writing these meditations. May their ministry of hospitality be filled with many blessings.

I am also grateful to Bishop William F. Murphy, STD, LHD, the bishop of my home diocese of Rockville Centre, NY, for his contribution to this book. I value him both as my bishop and as my friend.

Several prayerful people have written reflections on the Rosary as prayer. In thanking them I would also like to introduce them to you.

Loretta Tarter is married to Richard Tarter. They have five children and seven grandchildren. I recently celebrated Mass for her mother's 100th birthday. Philomena LaPolla prays the Rosary every day. Loretta is the business manager and secretary at Holy Cross Church in Nesconset, NY, where I am privileged to serve as pastor.

Sister Edward Joseph, CSJ, has been a Sister of St. Joseph of Brentwood, NY for over seventy years. She still volunteers in the parish office of Our Lady of Grace in West Babylon, NY, two days a week.

Barbara McGrellis and Tricia Callahan are directors of Faith Formation at Our Lady of Grace parish. Barbara and John McGrellis have two children; Tricia and Jim Callahan have three children. They are wonderful examples of lay ministry in the Church today.

Janet LaBorne lives in St. Martin of Tours in Amityville, NY, where she and her husband Jim raised

seven children. Jan has twenty grandchildren. She is gift-
ed in giving retreats and spiritual direction and has been a
great help to many people, including myself.

Msgr. Felix Machado is a priest from India who is
presently the undersecretary for the Pontifical Council for
Interreligious Dialogue. Felix has been my friend for twen-
ty-five years.

Denise Kretz and her husband Steven have four children and live in Amityville, NY. I witnessed their marriage
and baptized their children and have enjoyed their friendship since my ordination in 1971.

I am grateful for the gift of faith and the gift of priesthood that have brought me many blessings and much joy.

Contents

Foreword

THE LUMINOUS MYSTERIES, THE HOLY FATHER AND ME

This past summer it was my privilege to celebrate Mass for about 600 young people mostly from the United States but with some from other countries of Europe and Latin America. They were gathered, as Youth 2000, for a weekend of prayer and reflection on Mary in their lives. In my homily on Mary as the model and mirror of holiness, I confessed to them that I had a "bone to pick with the Holy Father." My reason was that, by providing us with the new Luminous Mysteries in his letter *Rosarium Viriginis Mariae* and suggesting we pray these mysteries on Thursdays, the Holy Father had completely upset the rhythm of my prayer life. From my childhood, I learned from my mother and older sister how to say the Rosary and what mysteries to reflect upon for each day of the week. Now I had to change all that and, at my age, I was constantly getting confused about which mysteries now belonged to what day of the week.

While this little story served to introduce a reflection on the richness of the mysteries of the Rosary and the many spiritual fruits that come to us from our meditation on the events in the life, death and resurrection of Our Lord through these mysteries, it does underscore an important point about the living out of our Catholic faith: Mary and the Rosary are an integral part of who we are as Catholics. All of us who were taught from childhood how to say the Rosary have been blessed to have this wondrous means of prayer as a formative and informative part of our very being as Catholics.

We know that, as we meditate on the events of our salvation from the Annunciation to the Coronation of Mary as Queen of Heaven, seeing these moments of salvation with Mary and from the perspective of Mary's love for her Son, gives us a deeper understanding of the depth and the breadth of God's love for us. Each mystery, seen through the eyes of that woman of faith, the first disciple of her Son, allows us to enter more intimately into Christ's saving love and be filled with an ever deeper sense of Him who has called us before we could name Him and who dwells in us so that we may ever dwell in Him. The Rosary, through the Joyful, Luminous, Sorrowful and Glorious Mysteries, is the most blessed of vehicles to bring Christ to us and us to Him.

We also know that the closer we come to Jesus through this "prayer that belongs to everyone," the closer we also come to Mary, the Mother of God and our Mother, the Mother of the Church. In his beautiful little book on his own priestly vocation, *Gift and Mystery,* Pope John Paul II tells us how St. Louis Grignion de Montfort helped him to understand this mutual enrichment of our spiritual lives. From the moment of the Annunciation, every aspect of Mary's life points to her son. Yet, the more deeply we see Him with the eyes of faith, the more surely He invites us to come closer to His mother, His first disciple, who, in a singular way, is the beginning of the Church, born from the side of Christ on the cross.

My conclusion with the young people of Youth 2000 was a simple one: I have no bone to pick with the Holy Father. Having given us the Luminous Mysteries, he has expanded the capacity of the Rosary to bring us closer to

Christ in His earthly ministry and to bring us closer to His mother as she accompanies Him in her earthly pilgrimage. Even more, we are united to her maternal heart as He is baptized in the Jordan, performs "the first sign" at Cana, preaches the Kingdom of God, is transfigured on Mount Tabor and gives to the apostles and the Church that "most precious gift" the Holy Eucharist.

I am grateful to my dear friend, Msgr. James McNamara, for this inspired series of reflections on the Rosary. As you and I continue to make the Rosary a central part of our life of prayer, I have every confidence that, meditating on these mysteries of the gospel message, we too will be able to say, "My soul magnifies the Lord; my spirit rejoices in God my savior."

—Most Reverend William Murphy
Bishop of Rockville Centre
August 27, 2003
Feast of St. Monica

Introduction

WHILE visiting Greccio in Italy where St. Francis of Assisi created the first Christmas crèche, I saw something carved over an ancient wooden doorway that said: "If the heart does not pray, then the tongue labors in vain."

I was taken with this statement as soon as I read it. I think it can be applied to many contexts. I will avoid the preacher's temptation to sermonize here and simply apply this bit of wisdom to the Rosary. "If the heart does not pray, then the tongue labors in vain." The Rosary is prayer, not the mechanical repetition of words. Prayer comes from the heart and is essentially adoration of God.

At the behest of our Holy Father, Pope John Paul II, we are celebrating the year of the Rosary. In his Apostolic Letter, *Rosarium Virginis Mariae*, Pope John Paul commends the Rosary to us as a form of contemplative prayer. In praying the Rosary he says we can contemplate with Mary the face of Christ. The Holy Father emphasizes that the Rosary is prayer; it is not simply the repetition of words. It is prayer that is based on Christ and on the Gospels.

Pope John Paul uses some truly memorable phrases that form the background to his teaching on the Rosary. The first is the directive Jesus gave to Peter at the shores of Lake Tiberias: *"Put out into the deep"* (Luke 5: 4). Peter was a fisherman. He knew the joys and the frustrations of his trade. He was learning to be an apostle and Jesus used what was familiar to him to get his attention. Peter put out into the deep and caught a great number of fish. In the

Church and the world today people of faith need to put out into the deep. We need to plunge ourselves into prayer and action in praise of God and in spreading God's Good News.

In beginning a new millennium of Christianity and ending a great Jubilee Year, John Paul was enthusiastic: *"Duc in altum (Put out into the deep)! These words ring out for us today and they invite us to remember the past with grati- tude, to live the present with enthusiasm and to look forward to the future with confidence: 'Jesus Christ is the same yesterday and today and forever'"* (Hebrews 13: 8).—*Novo Millennio Ineunte.*

It is in this spirit of gratitude, enthusiasm, and confi- dence that I begin these modest reflections upon the Mysteries of the Rosary. I begin with gratitude because the gifts of faith, family, and priesthood have formed my life in so much richness, more than money or possessions could ever provide. The older I get the more grateful I am for the people who have enriched my life, both living and deceased. Jesus Christ and His gospel way of life mean more to me now than ever before. I am grateful beyond words for the gift of faith and the gift of the Eucharist.

I begin with enthusiasm because I think that these extraordinary times in our Church and our world call for extraordinary responses. I do not claim to possess enthu- siasm. Rather, I beg God for the gift of enthusiasm. I remain happy as a priest even though I think it is harder to be a priest now than ever before. The recent scandals in the Church are part of this difficulty. But there are other challenges that have been increasing in recent years. Families are under greater pressure. In many families both parents are working. In some families one parent has sole responsibility for the family. The struggling economy, the crushing pace of modern life, the superficial narcissistic values of the culture, and the perceived irrelevance of the Church as an institution are further factors we face in trying to speak of God today. It is harder to get people's attention and to get them to give over their precious gift of time. They claim to be spiritual but not religious. This, in my opinion, leaves them rootless and wandering. Deeper prayer and an intense focus on Christ nourish my enthusiasm to win them over to Christ and to the Eucharist.

I begin with confidence because I truly believe that Jesus Christ is with us and will not abandon us. When I start worrying, I find much to worry about. I can worry about the changing habits of faith where many do not come to Mass on Sundays and some who do come do not come every week. I can worry about the Church, which has been suspect as an institution ever since institutions became suspect with Watergate and Vietnam and which is in crisis at the present time. I can worry about retirement, which seems less likely as the median age of priests rises. But all this worrying does me no good whatever because worrying distracts me from Christ and Christ is my confidence and my hope.

The other memorable phrase I wish to recall as we begin to look at the Rosary comes again from John Paul II. He says that the Rosary *"is a prayer of significance, destined to bring forth a harvest of holiness" (Rosarium Virginis Mariae)*. In the Church's rendezvous with springtime, a harvest of holiness is exactly what is called for at the present time. The Rosary, whether prayed alone or in community, is a contemplative prayer. Now, as soon as I say the Rosary is a contemplative prayer, I run the danger of losing readers who may immediately conclude that the Rosary is not meant for them because they are not contemplative. But contemplation is not limited to the monks in the monastery or the sisters in the cloister. Contemplation is the goal of all prayer and is, therefore, the way of prayer for all Christians.

To contemplate means to view or consider with continued attention, to gaze upon, to ponder. Contemplation simply means seeing what really is, appreciating reality not for what is obvious in our daily life but for what is hidden in the mystery of the presence and the love of Jesus in our fragile and passing world. Every one of us is called to contemplation. There are many paths of contemplation. The Rosary is one of them and a very good one. Centering Prayer (reverently repeating a sacred name for God), the Jesus Prayer *("Lord Jesus Christ, Son of the Living God, have mercy on me, a sinner."),* the spiritual exercises of St. Ignatius, and the use of Scripture in prayer are other worthwhile paths of contemplation. Each in themselves and all of these taken together are a harvest of holiness.

Through praying the Rosary we meditate upon the life of Jesus and the meaning of His life for our lives. We pray the Rosary. We do not simply say the Rosary. The Rosary is more than words said in a repetitive fashion. The Rosary is a means of entering into the mystery of Jesus by contemplating His life, death, and resurrection. Thus, the Rosary is centered on Jesus. Mary, the first disciple, the woman of extraordinary trust, can lead us to Christ through the Rosary. Mary was a contemplative woman throughout the unfolding drama of her Son's life. As we will see in the Joyful Mysteries, Mary often did not understand what was happening. After the visit of the shepherds to the stable Mary *"treasured all these things and pondered them in her heart"* (Luke 2: 19). Years later, when Jesus was lost in the temple and claimed to be about His Father's affairs, Mary and Joseph returned to the quiet life of Nazareth, and Mary *"treasured all these things in her heart"* (Luke 2: 51).

This contemplative stance of Mary throughout her life is a model for us in our own Christian living and in our praying the Rosary. There are many things we do not understand in this passing and incomplete world. The more we ponder the life of Christ, the more we become one with Him, even in the midst of our doubts and fears. The Rosary provides a contemplative way to ponder the life of Christ through the trust of Mary.

The Rosary is a beautiful prayer that everyone is encouraged to pray. The Rosary was developed some six hundred years ago as lay people sought a form of prayer that would fulfill their desire to pray. The fifteen decades were in imitation of the one hundred and fifty psalms of the Old Testament.

Adding the Luminous Mysteries, the Holy Father encourages us to pray the Rosary for peace in our terror-filled world, an urgent need today. Praying the Rosary is a great way to support people in need, for some special intention or in thanksgiving for blessings received.

Ordinary people have experienced extraordinary rewards by praying the Rosary, and so I have asked some prayerful people to offer their thoughts on the meaning of the Rosary in their lives. Interspersed throughout the reflections on the Mysteries of the Rosary you will find their witness to the Rosary as a valuable form of prayer. I recommend that you read these reflections in preparation for your own prayer.

Allow me to end the beginning with a story that expresses the true spirit of prayer: the spirit of expectation and hope. A woman called her pastor and asked him to visit her because she was quite ill and knew she would die soon. She told him a story and gave him instructions for her wake. She wanted him to place a fork in her hand when she was laid out in her coffin. The pastor smiled as he left from his visit. In a few months' time, the woman died. When her many friends and fellow parishioners came to her wake, they asked the pastor why she had a fork in her hands. He told them that the woman had gone to many dinners at the church. For years, whenever the volunteers came around to clear the tables before serving the dessert, they always said: "Keep your fork. The best is yet to come." The woman wanted the fork in her hand at her wake because she wanted everyone to know that the best was yet to come.

Reflections on the Rosary as Prayer

MY introduction to the Rosary was literally at my grandmother's knee. I used to visit my Nana each summer. The time she took in the afternoon to sit by her kitchen window in her rocking chair for a rest and to say the Rosary was the only time I saw her sitting all day. To accomplish this with a grandchild in tow, she had to include me in her activity. I sat on the footstool next to her rocker, and she taught me how to say the Rosary. She had 15-decade beads, little chaplets and the regular five-decade rosary and we'd finger the beads and say the Hail Marys and Our Fathers and spend time together. I looked forward every day to that time with her. Later in life when I didn't spend summers with her anymore and then when she died, I treasured those memories all the more.

She planted the seeds that flowered as I got older. I turned to the Rosary on my own and added the contemplative piece, meditating on the mysteries. I had a very deep devotion to the Blessed Mother, and as a teenager, this led me to discover St. Louis de Montfort's total consecration to Jesus through Mary. During this time of my young life, I attended daily Mass and the Rosary was the center of my prayer life. Meditating on the life of Jesus helped me make the decisions in life that are so difficult for everyone but especially for a teen and young adult. The Rosary was always a comfort to me. I prayed the Rosary when my father died, asking for strength to bear that pain. I prayed the Rosary for discernment and to thank God for being there to guide me. My family and I prayed the Rosary communally, saying it with our neighbors each week and with the parish Sodality. The Rosary was a link when I met my future husband. Our faith grew as we spent time together praying this simple prayer in the college chapel trying to discern our future.

Eventually I lost the fervor that marked my first twenty years. Devotion to Mary was becoming passé with the newfound freedoms and different focus of Vatican II. I found other ways to pray, and the prayer of my youth, seemed just that—a prayer for a young person, not the prayer of the mature adult I had become. I now meditated on Scripture; I read spiritual books; I plunged into liturgy; I attended prayer groups and discussion groups, but I didn't say the Rosary on a regular basis, even though I had never stopped carrying it with me and a rosary always hung on my bedpost.

Many years later I came back to the comfort prayer of my youth. I have accepted the fact that this prayer combines many types of prayer. I can be contemplative and reflective, and I can repeat the mantra of the Hail Mary. My devotion to Mary is not the devotion of my youth, but the devotion to Mary as the first disciple of Jesus. She really is my role model now more than ever, as I strive to live as a faithful disciple living out the Gospel. I am united to Jesus and able, through His grace, to think new thoughts while meditating on the same old mysteries. There is always room in my spiritual life for different kinds of prayer and prayer experiences, but I no longer think of the Rosary as only the prayer of my youth but as comfort food for my soul.   —*Loretta Tarter*

PRAYER to Our Blessed Mother through devotion to the Rosary is a very powerful prayer of intercession, and it is a source of great grace for those who pray it. This is not to be wondered at when considering the beautiful prayers composing it: the Apostles' Creed, the Lord's Prayer, the Hail Mary and the prayer which gives glory to the Most Holy Trinity. The concluding prayer of the Rosary is a prayer to Mary, Holy Queen, and Mother of Mercy. Each of the twenty decades of the Rosary is preceded by the mention of a Mystery of the life of Christ.

For hundreds of years this prayer has been said by the learned and the unlearned, the rich and the poor, adults and children. When the Mother of God appeared at Lourdes in France, and at Fatima in Portugal, thousands of people were present and were aware of Mary's urgent message to her children: "Pray the Rosary."

The Rosary is a vehicle which can greatly assist us on our journey home, our heavenly home. Why are we here on Earth? Why did God make us? It may be recalled that "God made us to know Him, to love Him, to serve Him in this world, and to be happy with Him forever in heaven." Heaven is our true home.

Through the power of the Holy Spirit, Our Blessed Mother brought Jesus into the world, here on planet Earth. She, indeed, knows the way that leads to Him. In her wisdom and great love for us she, desiring to guide us along the Way, has given us the Rosary.

Wise people carefully choose the necessary means to prepare them for a profession, vocation, career, physical health and/or whatever else they think will help them attain the lifestyle they would like to enjoy. In so doing, one should include the means leading to the home for which every human being has been created. There are many such means, one of which is the Rosary.

The reverent praying of the Rosary strengthens and deepens our faith, while making us aware of Mary's special relationship with God. She is the daughter of God the Father, mother of God the Son, and spouse of God the Holy Spirit, through whose power she conceived Jesus; and Mary is, of course, the temple of the Most Holy Trinity.

Can there be any doubt about the importance of the Rosary in our lives? Has the Mother of God ever come to her children on earth to urge them to recite any other prayer besides the Rosary?

Our Blessed Mother's personal appearance to her children urging the recitation of the Rosary is strong motivation for us. Yet beyond that is the need that we have to pray often. We need to know God and to love God. How do we get to know someone? Is it not through communication, or conversation? As we pray, the mystery of God's grace works within us, and works wonders!

Our Heavenly Father spoke one Word, Jesus. How do we respond to Jesus? It is easy to let days go by without thanking God for blessings of nature, of grace, of family, or of gifts that we don't even recognize as gifts. In fact, it is possible to be oblivious to God's presence in the world or in our lives as we hurry through each day's routine.

The daily recitation of the Rosary raises our awareness of the reality of Christ's life when He lived here more than 2,000 years ago. It gives meaning to some of His words that we may hear or read in Scripture. For example,

"Come to me . . . I will give you rest. Take my yoke upon you and learn from me because I am gentle and humble of heart and you will find rest."

Early morning is often the time of day chosen by people all over the world to walk or to do some other kind of exercise, or to meditate or contemplate.

Early in the morning is an excellent time to pray the Rosary. The silence and the uncluttered beauty of nature provides a perfect setting for raising our hearts and minds to our Creator to thank Him for this day and to ask His continued loving care of us. As a consequence of fidelity to this special devotion, one soon finds the "rest" of which Jesus speaks and enjoys the "peace which the world cannot give."

The Rosary is a wonderful and powerful form of prayer.

—*Sister Edward Joseph, CSJ*

Chapter 1

The Joyful Mysteries

THE Joyful Mysteries place before us significant events in the inception of the life of Christ. They are characterized by joy and they center on the person of Mary, the Mother of God and the first disciple of the beloved Son. These mysteries invite us to enter into a journey of discovery through Mary's heart. Since this journey is unique within all of history, I invite you to meditate upon these mysteries with a perspective of faith. In this way these events can surprise you because they are so rich. Instead of praying these mysteries as events of the past with which you are all too familiar, please join me in praying these mysteries with awe and reverence for what God is doing for His people through Mary and Elizabeth and through Jesus and John the Baptist.

A disciple is someone who follows Christ by first being in His company. Mary was the first disciple of Christ. She began to follow Jesus when she accepted the invitation to be the handmaid of the Lord. She was a unique disciple carrying Jesus in her womb. In praying these Joyful Mysteries, may we be disciples who enjoy the company of Jesus as much as Mary did, and may we prayerfully observe how Mary cooperated with God's plan and obeyed God's word.

The First Joyful Mystery: The Annunciation
Luke 1:26-38

A S Mary goes about her daily routine she pictures herself raising a family as the wife of the town carpenter. She is excited that her cousin Elizabeth has surprised the family with news that she is expecting a child and is already in her sixth month. Elizabeth's advanced age adds to the surprise, and her long desire to give birth increases the joy everyone is experiencing.

Mary senses that God is doing something new but she does not anticipate what happens on this quiet spring morning in Nazareth. The visit of the angel turns her life upside down, but Gabriel tells Mary not to fear. Fear is an obstacle to listening and to trusting the call of God.

Gabriel's words startle Mary. Who of us thinks we have won God's favor? How could she absorb what was being said, to say nothing of sorting out the many and varied feelings and fears welling up within her? Yet Gabriel invites her to step beyond her fears by trusting this message from God.

Her mind races ahead as she thinks of telling her parents and her betrothed and then of facing the rest of the people in her small town. There was much to fear within the culture and society of her time. Conception without marriage was a disgrace, punishable by stoning. But Mary moves from fear to faith because she trusts in God. She places herself in God's care with a resounding "yes" that reflects the enthusiasm of youth and the resiliency of faith: *"I am the handmaid of the Lord. Let what you have said be done to me"* (Luke 1:38).

In praying this first Joyful Mystery we can and should admire Mary. Mary is deserving of our reverence and respect. God uniquely graced Mary, preparing her for the special role she would play in God's plan for our salvation. However, in praying this mystery of the Annunciation, we cannot exempt ourselves from the unfolding drama by simply admiring Mary. What God asked of Mary in the Annunciation, God asks of us in our challenging world today. God calls us to be bearers of Christ; God invites us to move from fear to faith; God challenges us to trust in His promise to be with us and to sustain us.

It is true that God bestowed unique graces upon Mary but it is also true that God bestows unique graces upon us. Despite the tender background of September 11th and the horizon of terrorists' threats, God is still gracing us. In praying this Joyful Mystery, let us bring the drama of our lives with all our doubts, fears, and questions into our conversation with Christ. With the repetition of the Hail Mary, let us meditate on Mary's faith and trust and then move from fear to faith by seeking God through her intercession and in Christ's name.

In his Apostolic Letter, *Rosarium Virginis Mariae*, the Holy Father tells us that "the Rosary, though clearly Marian in character, is at heart a Christ-centered prayer." This is clearly evident in this first Joyful Mystery.

The Second Joyful Mystery: The Visitation
Luke 1:39-56

BEFORE the angel leaves Mary with the challenging news of the Annunciation, he tells her that Elizabeth had conceived a son through the providence of God "for nothing is impossible to God" (Luke 1:37).

This bit of information is very important for Mary. It sets her next course of action. Mary is not paralyzed by the news of the angel. She does not hide in Nazareth or shrink back in fear. She goes immediately to the one person with whom she can share this news and with whom she can face the future. What a moment of joy and excitement their meeting must have been. An elderly woman is marveling at the goodness of God, and a young woman is singing God's praises. This scene in itself is an apt description of praying the Rosary.

Mary and Elizabeth do not wait alone. They wait together. They wait together for the promises of God to be fulfilled. Elizabeth experiences the movement of the child in her womb. How overjoyed she must have been. She interprets the action of her unborn child as a leap of joy. This must have made both women wonder what God had in store for His people. They had, along with their whole nation, awaited the coming of the Messiah. And now it seemed that this promise was being fulfilled.

This second Joyful Mystery is indeed a prayer of joy. As you pray this mystery, allow yourself to be uplifted by Mary and Elizabeth. Allow your spirit to be raised from routine, discouragement or despair to enjoy the life and hope that are so radiant in the faces of these two beautiful women.

Elizabeth rejoices with Mary as they both appreciate what God is doing through them. They pray as faithful women of the Old Testament, but their prayers are not answered in the way they expect.

Many times in prayer we try to change God's perspective into ours. We pray for health and blessings for others and ourselves; we ask God for the gift of peace in our troubled world. These are good things and we are right to pray prayers of petition and intercession as we do when we pray the Rosary. The problem is not what we pray for but how we pray. We try to change God's perspective into ours, to get God to do things our way. But what we really need to ask God for is to change our perspective into His. In prayer we seek to take on the mind of Christ. All prayer is an exercise in faith and trust where we surrender our limited perspective to the providence of God.

Thus the compliment that Elizabeth gives Mary is instructive for us. She said that Mary was blessed because she trusted that the promise God made to her would be fulfilled. For years Elizabeth tried to change God's perspective. She prayed that she might conceive and bear a child. She not only wanted to be a mother, she wanted to be released from the shame her barrenness brought upon her. Now in her old age she is given the gift she had stopped praying for in her advanced years. Now she surrenders her perspective to God's providence as she rejoices that nothing is impossible to God.

Mary sings her trust and surrender in the hymn of praise we call *The Magnificat*. She knows in her soul that God has done great things for her and that God has exalted the lowly. She praises God's holy name and proclaims God's mercy.

This second Joyful Mystery holds the key to prayer. In praying this second Joyful Mystery, I invite you to place your trust in Christ and to surrender your will to His will just as Mary did. Allow Christ to walk with you in the unfolding drama of your own life as you face the uncertainties of youth or the challenges of aging. As you pray the Rosary, do not walk alone. Walk with Jesus and with Mary.

Mary stayed with Elizabeth just long enough for Elizabeth to give birth to John the Baptist. They waited together, not alone. They enabled each other to wait. They waited from promise to fulfillment, not from nothing to something, because they waited in faith and trust.

How are you waiting upon God and who are your companions in this waiting? When you pray in faith and trust, you never pray alone.

The Third Joyful Mystery: The Birth of Christ
Luke 2:1-20

WHEN Mary returned from her visit with Elizabeth she could feel the new life beginning within her womb. Joseph took her as his wife after being drawn into the plan of salvation that was unfolding. Joyful anticipation marked their days.

When the time drew near, Mary and Joseph set out for Bethlehem. Travel by donkey over rough roads was arduous in the best of circumstances and truly difficult in the late stages of pregnancy. In praying this third Joyful Mystery, we are invited to journey with Mary and Joseph on this very difficult venture. We might unite our struggles and burdens with Mary and Joseph as they move closer to their time of joy in the birth of this precious child. God graced them and God was with them but this did not mean that life would be easy. The journey to Bethlehem in itself was a hardship.

Sometimes we naively think that if we pray and try to live a holy life, our life should be free from difficulty. This leads to discouragement. But prayer does not shield us from the difficulties of this life. Through prayer we exercise our faith and by exercising our faith we become stronger in the face of the adversities of this life. In praying this Joyful Mystery we might not only meditate on the birth of Jesus but also on the journey of Mary and Joseph to get to Bethlehem. God was with them in the difficulty of the journey as well as in the joy of Christ's birth.

You might pray the first half of this decade by meditating on the long journey of Joseph and Mary and then pray the second half by experiencing the joy of the birth of

Christ. Joy and pain are often intertwined in our lives. A child is born soon after the loss of a loved one. Parents face health problems even as they anticipate the marriage of a son or daughter. Thus we learn to enjoy life despite the difficulties. God shows us this in the way Jesus was born.

The very circumstances of the birth of Christ reveal the extent of God's love and humility. In the spontaneous movement of love that led to the decision that the Son would enter human life, Jesus could have come in any form and under any circumstances He wished. He could have come on earth as a powerful king or a wealthy lord.

Jesus chooses to come among us as a vulnerable infant. He chooses the circumstances of a cold stable where only the natural warmth of animals gives Him comfort. He becomes an outcast by the edict of Herod to destroy each firstborn male so as to eliminate this child whom Herod sees as a threat.

We learn something about God through these circumstances of Christ's birth. We learn through this powerful example that God is love. God does not simply love. God is the very essence of love. There is no condescension in Christ entering human life. There is unconditional love. The profound humility of God flows from this unconditional love.

We also learn something about ourselves when Christ enters human life. We learn that Jesus identifies with us in our weakness and in our vulnerability. We would like to think that we are in control of this life. We save for the future and take out insurance for contingencies. These are good and prudent things to do. But deep down we know that we are not in control of this life. Our health could fail tomorrow. We could face disaster even though we try so hard to avoid it.

It is clear that our God wants to be with us when we are most in need, when we are at our lowest point, when we have reason to fear. This is true in the birth of Christ as well as in His death on Calvary.

As we pray this third Joyful Mystery we might pray with appreciation of Mary, Joseph, and Jesus. We might pray with appreciation of Mary and Joseph as they continued to trust in God's promise of a safe delivery of this child who *"will be great and will be called the Son of the Most High"* (Luke 1:32). In the midst of the arduous travel and the many unknowns they faced, Mary and Joseph must have been tempted to doubt God. But they did not doubt. They trusted God.

In the midst of our difficulties we are tempted to doubt God. In appreciation of Mary and Joseph let us trust God not only when all ends well but also in the midst of difficulty. Praying in this way will make our faith stronger.

Let us also pray this Joyful Mystery in appreciation of Jesus. We join the shepherds and the wise men from the East in paying homage to Jesus. Let us place our trust in Jesus who so completely entrusted Himself to us in a cold stable in Bethlehem.

The Fourth Joyful Mystery: The Presentation of Jesus in the Temple
Luke 2:21-38

SOON after the birth of Jesus, Mary and Joseph had to flee into Egypt because the insecure Herod issued an edict that the first-born son of each family be killed. Herod's aim was to eliminate Christ. Thus, Jesus became an illegal immigrant, the target of jealousy on the part of the ruling authority.

Can you imagine the fear that Mary and Joseph experienced when they fled their native land until this storm of destruction passed by? Can you appreciate their faith when they return to God the gift they have been given in the birth of their Son?

Once again we are invited in our prayer to be part of the unfolding human drama. This is indeed a joyous occasion. They consecrate Jesus to the Lord and they offer a sacrifice in thanksgiving. As often happens in our own lives, moments of pure joy can be traced with sorrow or hint of impending pain. This joyful moment is interrupted by two elderly devout people who prophesy an ominous future for the child and His mother.

We can best pray this fourth Joyful Mystery from a parental perspective as Mary and Joseph receive the praise and the prophesy of Simeon and Anna. Simeon thanks God that he has lived to see this child whom he praises as *"a light to the nations and the glory of your people Israel"* (Luke 2:32). Before Mary and Joseph can begin to comprehend the meaning of these words, Simeon speaks to a mother's heart: *"You see this child: he is destined for the fall and the ris-*

ing of many in Israel, destined to be a sign that is rejected—and a sword will pierce your own soul too—so that the secret thoughts of many may be laid bare" (Luke 2:34-35). Anna then enters the scene, praises God and prophesies that the child will be the means of the deliverance of Jerusalem.

The scene ends abruptly. Mary and Joseph return to Nazareth with much in their hearts to sort out. Do you think they shared their confusion and their fear with each other, wondering what Simeon meant by his praise and his prophesy and what Anna was trying to say? When you face uncertainty, do you share it with a spouse or a friend or do you carry it alone?

This is the beginning of a deeper contemplative journey for Mary and Joseph. They had already been pondering in their hearts the meaning of the annunciation and the birth of Jesus. Now their hearts are heavy with the words of praise and prophesy they have heard in the temple. These words would stay with them forever. Mary stores them in her heart. This is truly a maternal form of contemplation. What mother has not stored in her heart the things she does not understand or her fears for the welfare of her children? What father has not wondered at some point what he might have done differently? What friend has not pondered the mystery and freedom of love in relationship?

❧

Often enough both praise and the prediction of doom, while seeming so different from each other, can leave us wondering what was meant or what the future holds. In praying this fourth Joyful Mystery we are invited to walk with Mary and Joseph as they face an unknown future. What does it mean that this child will be the glory of the people Israel? What is the sword that will pierce Mary's soul? When will this happen?

When we pray there is a subtle temptation to want to control life, to get God to do what we want. In praying this fourth Joyful Mystery we are invited to ponder the mystery of joy and sorrow. We are not in control of this life. We are in the providential care of God just as the Holy Family was long ago.

In this fourth Joyful Mystery as well as in the fifth, we are given the opportunity to ponder the many things in our lives that are beyond our comprehension. We can best do this by uniting our hearts with Mary and Joseph. No matter what happens to them, no matter the challenges they face or the joys they experience, they know that God is with them and so they store these events in their hearts in order to find meaning and experience peace.

Their experience is similar to our experience. No matter what happens to us, God is with us even if we do not feel His presence, even if we doubt His existence. To find God in the difficulty of the journey, in the joy of the moment, in the fear of terrorism or in the practice of our faith, we need to store these moments in our hearts and, like Mary and Joseph, wait patiently for meaning and peace.

The Fifth Joyful Mystery: The Finding of Jesus in the Temple
Luke 2:41-52

THE last Joyful Mystery is also a moment beyond our comprehension. Mary will store this experience in her heart as she attempts to understand her Son and the prophesy of Simeon that a sword will pierce her soul.

Life seems to have gone along with some regularity and routine for a dozen years as Mary and Joseph settled into Nazareth. That routine would include arduous household tasks for Mary and carpentry for Joseph. By now Jesus was old enough to be involved in the carpentry shop. He was probably fascinated by His father's skills and thrilled to learn this trade alongside such a special mentor.

At the same time Jesus knows this is not enough and that His destiny far surpasses the small town of Nazareth and a career as a carpenter. This becomes evident in the visit to Jerusalem as Jesus moves toward maturity. Joseph and Mary go to Jerusalem in gratitude for God's deliverance of His people. They go in remembrance of the time when the homes of the people marked with the blood of the lamb were passed over by the destructive plague.

There is a sense of comfort and community in the description of a caravan of families traveling together. If Jesus is not with them, he must be with one of the other families. It is natural for a twelve-year-old boy to be with a friend. So Mary and Joseph proceed on their journey for three days before they realize Jesus is not in the caravan.

I cannot imagine the terror that pervaded their hearts as they realized that their Son was missing. Mary, the beautiful Lady who bore Jesus into our midst, had already learned to ponder the mysteries of God's ways in her heart. As any parent knows from the birthing to the letting go, Mary knows that her Son does not belong to her.

Now Jesus is missing and Mary wonders if this is the sword that Simeon predicted would pierce her soul. A mother's uncertainty, her fear for her son, is lived out in the frenetic return to Jerusalem and the frantic search of the temple. Is He alive? Has something terrible happened to Him? Has someone taken Him? Oh God, where is my Son?

Jesus was missing. He was lost for three days, three days that seemed to contain a lifetime. Finally, they found Him in the temple. Despite their relief, they asked Him why He had wounded them with such anxiety and fear. The answer He gave is true but is beyond their comprehension: another thing to ponder in their hearts.

Jesus was in the temple being true to Himself. He was being Jesus. In the midst of the elders and the teachers, He was being true to his vocation as the Holy One of God, sent to bring glad tidings to the poor, to set captives free, to proclaim a year of favor from the Lord. Jesus was being the Christ, the Son of the living God. And Mary pondered all these things in her heart until she stood in the shadow of the cross and finally experienced the sword that pierced her soul and that brought us salvation.

In praying this fifth decade of the Rosary, we might ask Mary to touch our hearts with her maternal wisdom. We too ponder many things in our hearts that we do not understand. The terrible events of September 11th still resound in our hearts. Questions about injustice in our world between nations and between people still weigh upon our minds.

While Mary and Joseph experienced the joy of finding Jesus, they also knew the anguish and fear of searching for Him. This left them with some searing questions to ponder. We also know anguish and fear. We too are left with searing questions to ponder. Sometimes our anguish and fear are realized in a tragic ending. Our anger can separate us from God when we blame God for the death of a loved one or the experience of great evil. Before we turn to the Mysteries of Light, we might need to express our anger to God so that we can enter into a real relationship with Jesus. Then we can join Jesus as He goes about His Father's affairs. He walks among us, suffers with us, heals us, and loves us.

For now, let us rejoice with Mary and Joseph who embrace their Son and carry in their hearts all that they do not understand about Him.

Reflections on the Rosary as Prayer

ONE may ask what the Rosary can offer us in the twenty-first century. What value would there be in learning to pray this way? Just the other day I was talking to a friend of mine who had just lost her business. She was angry, confused and struggled with feelings of betrayal and failure. She was searching for something to hold on to so that she could keep her Christian dignity in the face of overwhelming hurt. She needed peace and perspective and so I told her this story . . .

For as far back as I can remember I have prayed the Rosary. My parents made it an integral part of our lives. We prayed the Rosary as a family and it taught us to rely on prayer as a means of solace and surrender. The Rosary was the one prayer that you could say, the one thing you could do when life left you mute and paralyzed in the face of life's most tragic and triumphant moments. It was a gift from loving parents who knew about life's unexpected twists and turns and how important it was to hang on and trust in God. The Rosary and its mysteries remind us that Jesus and Mary were completely immersed in our human experience and that they too had to hang on and trust in God the Father. This knowledge helped us to connect our ordinary lives to the divine plan.

As I repeat over and over again, "Hail Mary full of grace the Lord is with you, blessed are you among women and blessed is the fruit of your womb, Jesus," I am reminded of the awesome love our God has for us. I'm reminded of that moment when Mary said "yes" despite her unknowing. It was by making herself available to God that Jesus became tangible and available to us. I'm reminded of Elizabeth's recognition of God alive and living in another human being. I'm reminded that our God would do anything to be close to us even if it meant becoming a creature himself to show us the way. In this simple repetitive prayer along with the Our Father and Glory Be my consciousness is awakened to the presence of God and His intimate connection to us.

Although the Rosary is a Catholic tradition, it is faithful to our universal origins. It encompasses all the finest prayer forms from around the world. It is beautifully inclusive of our senses on a human level and of religious diversity on a cultural level. It includes prayer beads and meditation common in Eastern religions and devotional and scripturally-based forms common to Western religions.

However, I believe its greatest asset lies in its contemplative nature. It allows us to slow down, get into a rhythm, which is something that is lacking in our society and culture today. Like a gardener who first prepares the soil for planting, this repetitive rhythm prepares our hearts for an encounter with God. The ebb and flow of words and images helps us to meditate on the life of Jesus and Mary, which always points to the love story between God and His creation. It is a prayer that is steeped in the hope that our God does not exist up in the clouds but that our God is with us in the muck and mire, joy and elation in our own lives.

The Rosary has transformative power. As I grow and experience the ups and downs of life, the Rosary and the mysteries it contains takes on different meaning. It is comforting and consoling, challenging and uplifting. It is a part of my Catholic heritage that stands true and sure like a beacon of hope in a chaotic and sometimes frightening world. When I pray I float in the love of God and become renewed and grounded.

To some the Rosary may seem old, simply beads on a string but to me it is a portal to encounter God. Its beauty lies in its simplicity and accessibility to all. The real challenge with the Rosary or any prayer is to choose to spend time with God. In choosing to spend time with God praying the Rosary we, the pilgrims of the twenty-first century, will find peace for our hearts, hope for the future and the awareness of God's love and presence in our lives.

—*Barbara McGrellis*

A S I began to reflect on the Rosary as prayer, I found myself reaching for my rosary beads. As I did, I automatically clutched them to my heart! That says something to me. Primarily it says my heart is touched when I say the rosary prayers. I have a long history with this way of praying—since I was a young woman. In those days I prayed mostly in petition and thanksgiving. But as I look back now over the years, I realize how praying the Rosary opened me up to other kinds of prayer that I would, in time, find so fulfilling. I love to pray the scriptural rosary—each bead of the Hail Marys has a quote from Scripture on which to meditate.

Meditating on the life of Christ through the Rosary leads me into the contemplation of how my Christ lived and loved and died and rose again and is forever with me.

In my prayerful imagination I am there with Christ. And the endless benefits of this closeness cannot ever be tabulated. Yes, this is what touches my heart.

I have been with Christ at birth—the wonder of our God manifesting Himself in the most lovable and adorable form—a baby. And the prayer continues every time I see or hold a baby and am reminded of the wonder of our God. The life of Christ comes alive in the ordinariness of my own life. My husband and I raised seven children and now have twenty grandchildren. I've loved a lot of babies—up close and personal.

There are those times I prayed the Rosary as a mantra. I remember the words of St. Paul as he reminds us that: "The Spirit comes to help us in our weakness. For when we cannot choose words in order to pray properly, the Spirit himself expresses our plea in a way that could never be put into words" (Romans 8:26). There were times when I didn't think I could pray, when a desolate weariness overcame me, or anxieties or fear. But I needed to stay in God's presence—and I fingered the rosary beads and repeated the words to keep me focused on my Christ, with the help of Mary who blessedly hovers. As the pain in my own life opened me to the sorrowful mysteries of Christ's life, I never felt alone. I had that strong sense of companionship with the One who's been there—knows the pain and comforts me from the depth of an understanding heart. And I am drawn deeper into that heart—the heart of Christ.

I want nothing more than to adapt my heart to Christ's heart. I want the rhythm of our hearts to be one.

—*Janet LaBorne*

Chapter 2

The Mysteries of Light

OUR Holy Father, Pope John Paul II, proclaimed October 2002 to October 2003 the year of the Rosary, and he offered to the Church a new set of mysteries of the Rosary. He has not changed the Rosary, which remains the same meditative structure of five decades consisting of one Our Father and ten Hail Marys for each decade. The Holy Father has simply added a new series of events from the life of Christ to enrich our praying of the Rosary.

We are familiar with the Joyful, the Sorrowful, and the Glorious Mysteries of the Rosary. They recount and remember key events at the bookends in the life of Jesus and Mary. The new mysteries of the Rosary are full of life and hope. They are appropriately called the Mysteries of Light and they fill in a missing part of the existing mysteries. The Joyful Mysteries unfold for us the beginning of Christ's life. The Sorrowful Mysteries reveal God's saving love at the end of Christ's life. And the Glorious Mysteries proclaim the new life of Christ risen from the dead. The Mysteries of Light lay out the key events in the life and ministry of Christ.

I find these new mysteries to be abounding in hope and faith. The Mysteries of Light are: The Baptism of Jesus, the Wedding Feast of Cana, the Proclamation of the Kingdom of God, the Transfiguration on Mount Tabor, and the Institution of the Eucharist.

The new mysteries of the Rosary will shed light on the way of Christ that alone leads to the fullness of life. They are destined to bring forth a harvest of holiness.

The First Mystery of Light: The Baptism of Jesus in the Jordan River

Matthew 3:13-17

THE first Mystery of Light is rich in symbolism and meditation for us as we pray the Rosary. All the mysteries of light reveal the Kingdom of God in the person of Jesus Christ. Each event in the life of Christ gives a glimpse of the Kingdom that awaits us in the holy presence of God. Jesus is the very presence of that Kingdom in His person and in His saving actions.

This is beautifully expressed in the baptism of Jesus. As you prepare to pray this Mystery of Light you might first read the account of Christ's Baptism in the Gospels: Matthew 3:13-17, Mark 1:9-11, and Luke 3:21-22. In each Gospel the account itself is quite simple. Jesus suddenly arrives at the Jordan River where John the Baptist has been preparing the people. Amidst the chaos of a jostling crowd anxious for hope, John the Baptist must have been startled to see Jesus approaching him in the water.

How humble of Jesus to seek baptism by John! The people probably quieted down as they saw John staring at Christ. As so often happens in our lives, Jesus was in their midst but they did not yet have an appreciation of Him. In Matthew's account John the Baptist expresses his unworthiness to baptize Jesus, feeling that Jesus should baptize him. Jesus assures him that this is His desire.

The people—anxious for hope—are given a glimpse into the person of Christ. As Jesus emerges from the water the Spirit of God comes upon Him in the visible form of a dove and proclaims for all to hear: "You are my Beloved

Son; with you I am well pleased" (Mark 13: 11). This is the Jesus we contemplate as we pray the Rosary: the Beloved Son on whom God's favor rests. We will see this glimpse of God again in the fourth Mystery of Light when Jesus is transfigured on Mount Tabor in the presence of three privileged friends.

The people at the Jordan River must have been startled and confused by this mysterious event. As the ministry of Jesus unfolded, much attention would be given to what Jesus said and did. Controversy would soon mark the work of Christ as Jesus came into conflict with those who had the largest investment in religious matters. Some would never come to appreciate the person of Christ.

Praying the Rosary is an opportunity to appreciate the person of Christ, not simply what He says and what He does but who He is. The Rosary is a path to contemplation. The real goal of all prayer is contemplation and the goal of contemplation is to simply be in the presence of Jesus Christ. In this context you can see the importance of appreciating the person of Jesus, the most beautiful person who ever walked the face of the earth.

ᏚᏬ

In the process of praying the Rosary with this first Mystery of Light, it is good to reflect upon the humble approach of Jesus at the Jordan. Through the repetition of the Hail Mary, allow the disarming humility of Christ to seep into your consciousness. Here is Jesus the Christ, the Holy One of God, kneeling in front of John the Baptist and being submerged in the waters.

A harvest of holiness can be found in contemplating Jesus as He emerges from the waters of the Jordan River.

From the human perspective of those privileged to be present, Jesus enters the waters of John's baptism an unknown son of a carpenter from Nazareth. He emerges from the water anointed by the Spirit of God as the Beloved Son and proclaimed to all present as the fulfillment of their hopes.

The heavenly Father delights in Jesus by the Jordan River just as He will delight in Jesus on Mount Tabor. The Father delights in you and me as we seek to follow His path of love. In this first Mystery of Light we are given insight into the person of Jesus as the Beloved Son. In praying this first Mystery of Light, let us appreciate Jesus and let us realize how much our God appreciates us.

The Second Mystery of Light: The Self-manifestation of Jesus at the Wedding of Cana
John 2:1-12

THE second Mystery of Light is found only in John's Gospel and it is John's way of beginning the public ministry of Jesus. In praying this mystery of the Rosary our attention is directed to Mary who gives Jesus a nudge to go forth.

Jesus is at the wedding reception with some of his newly called disciples. Such a joyous occasion would have provided an opportunity for them to get to know one another in a relaxed atmosphere. Jesus is just emerging from the silent life of Nazareth. In John's account Jesus has not yet made a speech or performed a miracle. He has simply gathered five ordinary working people to join Him in an enterprise that would indeed change the world.

They run out of wine at the wedding, surely an embarrassment for the host and hostess. It is Mary who intervenes. Mary is the first disciple of Jesus. She has nurtured him in Nazareth and she will be there, silently following throughout the ministry that will fill the next three years. With a woman's intuition and a mother's heart, Mary goes directly to Jesus. The exchange between them is intriguing. Mary tells Jesus they have no wine. His reply is not what we might expect: *"Woman, why turn to me? My hour has not come yet"* (John 2:4). Jesus is referring to the hour of his glorification when all of His life and ministry will be summed up by His death and resurrection. The timing of that hour is at the behest of the Father. Once again we see the humility of Jesus as He seeks to follow the path the Father has placed before Him. We believe that Jesus was like us in all things except sin. Thus, in His human nature He grew into a full realization of the path He was to take and the mission He was to fulfill.

Mary does not hesitate because her intuition and her heart tell her something else. They tell her that the time has come for her Son to go forth. Recall that when Jesus was lost in the temple at the age of twelve, Mary did not understand Jesus' explanation that He had to be about His Father's affairs. She knew her Son was unique and that a drama of salvific proportions would one day unfold but, for all those intervening years, she simply stored these things in her heart and pondered them. It is out of this contemplation that Mary acts at the wedding in Cana. *"Do whatever He tells you."* In effect Mary says to Jesus: "It is time for you to be about your Father's affairs. Go now and explode with divine love upon the earth."

What a marvelous moment! What a great fruit of prayer and contemplation! Mary, the simple, young woman who bore the Savior into our world, now gives Him a nudge to perform a sign of the new things that are to come. Jesus accepts Mary's directive and changes the water into wine. The words of the Hail Mary are apt for this scene at Cana: *"Hail Mary, full of grace, the Lord is with you."* Mary is full of grace when she challenges Jesus at the wedding at Cana.

☙

In addition to considering Mary's courage, there is another dimension of this story worthy of our reflection when we pray the Rosary. The first thing Jesus did before beginning His public ministry was to gather a community to walk with Him. He does not go about His mission of love alone. From the outset He gathers a community. In the context of the individualism of our culture and the disillusionment with our Church, there is a tendency and a temptation to go it alone today. People say they want God but not religion; they seek spirituality but not Church.

There are enormous pitfalls to this approach. In a me-and-God spirituality, God ends up being anything I make Him to be and can simply be a projection of my own needs and whims. Without a tradition (a community going back in time) and a Church (a community in the present) I do not believe that faith is sustainable or healthy. Our Church is not perfect and we know that now more than ever before, but it is the sacrament of our salvation instituted by Jesus Christ.

Thus, it is instructive for us that, from the very beginning, Jesus gathered a community to walk with Him and to whom He would entrust His message and mission. When we pray we never pray alone. Whether we pray by ourselves or with others, in the midst of the Eucharist or in the solitude of our room, we are praying with others, with a community of believers and followers of the way of Christ.

The Rosary, then, is a communal prayer whether we pray it by ourselves or in common. It is a harvest for holiness in the Church today. In praying this second Mystery of Light, let us ask Mary to lead us closer to Christ, the Son she nudged into action for our salvation.

The Third Mystery of Light: Jesus Proclaims the Kingdom of God and Calls Us to Conversion
Mark 1:14-15

BEFORE beginning any of the decades of the Rosary, it is valuable to spend a few minutes thinking about the mystery at hand. Here it is the nearness of God's Kingdom in the person of Jesus Christ. He proclaims a Kingdom of love and He calls us to conversion. In order to respond wholeheartedly and enthusiastically, we first immerse ourselves in the person of Jesus Christ. If we even get a glimpse into the beautiful person of Jesus Christ, conversion will come easily, even naturally.

The Good News that Jesus proclaims is first and foremost about what God has done and is doing for us, not what we do for God. The Kingdom of God is close at hand because Jesus is here. Indeed, God is here and God isn't going to go away. This is the Good News. If we believe this Good News, then we can repent. We repent; we change; and we turn around because God is doing something unique. *"This is the love I mean: not our love for God but God's love for us when He sent His Son to take our sins away . . . We are to love, then, because He loved us first"* (1 John 4:10, 19).

Everything that follows in the ministry of Jesus and in the Christian era is based in this message: *"The time has come and the Kingdom of God is close at hand. Repent, and believe the Good News."* The Kingdom of God can seem a mere abstraction, far off in the future. Yet the Kingdom of God begins here and now in the person of Jesus Christ.

The Kingdom of God is an experience of harmony with God in a life beyond the bounds of space and time. It is also an experience beyond our ability to comprehend in this life. The Kingdom of God is centered in the person of Jesus Christ. Once again, in praying the Rosary in this Mystery of Light, the goal is contemplation, an experience beyond words into the eloquence of silence. Our closest experience to this is the experience of being with a beloved spouse or friend. Sometimes there are no words that can express the joy of being together and the experience of being one in heart and spirit.

God initiates all Christian living. It is God who calls. It is God who comes. It is God who invites. It is Jesus who begins His ministry with the proclamation that the Kingdom of God is near. Our Christian lives are in response to God calling, coming, and inviting. This is the center of the preaching of Jesus.

In praying this mystery of the Rosary we are invited to focus our attention on this Gospel core of proclamation and call.

The call to conversion is a call to order and/or reorder our lives in response to the marvelous love God is sharing with us. But first we need to be caught up in God's marvelous love. If we are not captured by God's love, our Christian living will be about our own justification or our feeble attempts to prove to God that we love Him.

Like a sport's fan wildly enthusiastic about a beloved team, we are invited in this third Mystery of Light to be wildly enthusiastic about the victory of good over evil, the triumph of life over death in the person and the action of Jesus Christ. Out of this perspective and in response to what God continues to do for us, a harvest of holiness will spring forth.

The Fourth Mystery of Light: The Transfiguration
Luke 9:28-36

THE Transfiguration is believed to have taken place on Mount Tabor. Several years ago I gave a retreat on Mount Tabor to Franciscan priests serving in the Holy Land. It was a tremendous privilege to be on Mount Tabor for six days. The view from Mount Tabor is a panorama of valleys and countryside in that ancient Biblical land. It is easy to see why Mount Tabor is considered the site of the Transfiguration.

Pope John Paul II calls the Transfiguration the Mystery of Light *par excellence.* In praying the Rosary through this fourth Mystery of Light, we have a unique opportunity to be caught up in the beauty of God. Before praying this decade of the rosary, spend a few moments imaging the scene that unfolds on the mountain (Matthew 17:1-9, Mark 9:2-10, Luke 9:28-36). Jesus takes Peter, James, and John up the mountain to spend some time in prayer. He singles them out from the band of twelve whom He has called to form the first community of disciples.

They must have felt very privileged to be invited by Jesus to be with Him when He went off to pray. But then something happens that is truly remarkable. As Jesus prays He is transfigured before their very eyes. They experience Jesus in the context of His divinity, standing with Moses and Elijah. The Gospel writers tell us that His face was changed and His garments radiated the brilliance of lightning.

This is a moment of great intimacy in the deepening relationship between Jesus and His closest friends. The intimacy of their relationship yields insight into the person of Jesus. In a brief moment they would like to prolong, they see Jesus as He really is: the perfect gift of the Father to all of humanity and the perfect expression of all that is good in human nature. Anyone who has experienced the gift of friendship and the intimacy of unconditional love has some appreciation of what Peter, James, and John experienced on Mount Tabor.

Peter expresses the sentiments of all three when he wants to make the moment last forever by building a monument to what they have seen. But the moment doesn't last forever. Rather, the moment passes into the flow of days and they return to the routine of daily life. Their experience must have been both a blessing and a burden. Surely, the experience in itself is a blessing, a moment they will treasure and that will enlighten and encourage them at other times like Gethsemane and Calvary. Here is the burden: telling no one what they have seen—holding this experience in the silence of their hearts.

The Transfiguration is a religious experience for Peter, James, and John. As such, it is a blessing and a burden. This is true of most religious experiences. In prayer we are always seeking God. There are moments (though they are rare) when we feel God's presence in a particularly personal way or are overwhelmed by God's unconditional love for us. In itself, this is a blessing but there is also a burden that can take several forms. One burden is the experience of trying to express to others what seems too ineffable for words. Another burden is the challenge to integrate this religious moment into our daily living. A third burden is the tendency to compare all subsequent experiences in prayer to the Tabor experience that so touched our hearts.

All is gift. All is grace. The only proper response to a gift is gratitude. The gift becomes a burden when we turn the gift into an expectation. Instead of being grateful for the gift we have received, we want God to do it again and again. We judge subsequent prayer by the Tabor moment and we become discouraged instead of grateful.

In praying this fourth decade of the Mystery of Light, we might enter the scene and simply be there with Jesus. The more we can let go of our expectations and allow Christ to be Christ, the more we can appreciate Jesus. Once again, this is what contemplation is all about. Praying the Rosary is a form of contemplative prayer.

One of the hallmarks of the Christian life is surrender. The key to prayer and to contemplation is surrender. In order to love others we often need to forgive them. In order to forgive them we need to surrender, to let go of our hurts and disappointments. A similar dynamic is at work in prayer. In order to pray we need to surrender, to let go of our expectations, our desire to be in control (to be God) and allow God to be God. God will speak to us in His time not ours, in the mystery of His love, not in answer to our expectations.

A harvest of holiness was seeded on Mount Tabor long ago when Peter, James, and John treasured the moment and surrendered it to the flow of days. We can do no better than to do the same.

The Fifth Mystery of Light: The Institution of the Eucharist

Matthew 26:26-29; 1 Corinthians 11:23-26

IT is fitting that the last Mystery of Light is the Eucharist. All the Mysteries of Light highlight key events in the life and ministry of Jesus. The entire meaning of the life and mission of Jesus is given to us in the Eucharist. The Eucharist is not some static entity or simply a means of remembering what Jesus did long ago. The Eucharist is the living and vibrant action of Jesus Christ here and now.

The most critical catechetical need in the Church today is an appreciation of the meaning and importance of the Eucharist for Christian living. The total self-giving of Christ is the core of the Eucharist. Jesus gave Himself totally for us at one point in time on Calvary. Jesus continues to give Himself totally to us in each Eucharist that we celebrate. The Eucharist is the greatest gift God gives us in our Catholic Church.

Because the Eucharist is an activity full of God's love, it demands our participation, not simply our attendance. Therefore, it is not proper to pray the Rosary during Mass. Meditation upon the mystery of gift and grace in the Eucharist is proper when praying the Rosary.

The institution of the Eucharist is recounted in the first three Gospels. The account given by St. Paul in the first letter to the Corinthians is a testimony of faith: *"For this is what I received from the Lord and in turn pass on to you: that on the same night that He was betrayed, the Lord Jesus took some bread and thanked God for it and broke it and He said: 'This is my Body which is for you; do this as a memorial of me.'*

In the same way He took the cup after supper and said: 'This cup is the new covenant in my Blood. Whenever you drink it, do this as a memorial of me.' Until the Lord comes, therefore, every time you eat this bread and drink this cup, you are proclaiming His death" (1 Corinthians 11:23-26).

In the first and the fourth Mysteries of Light, the Spirit descends upon Jesus and proclaims for all to hear that Jesus is the Beloved Son on whom God's favor rests. In the Eucharist Jesus is giving Himself to us in the same act of generosity that marked His total gift of self on Calvary. We can appreciate that Jesus was the Beloved Son at the Jordan River in the moment of baptism and on Mount Tabor at the moment of insight and intimacy. We have no problem seeing that God's favor rested upon Him at those moments. But it is hard for us to see that Jesus was the beloved Son in the Garden of Gethsemane and on the Cross of Calvary. We tend to think that Jesus is the victim of the Father's will on the Cross. We picture the Father as sending Jesus to Calvary. But Jesus is still the Beloved Son in the anguish of the Garden and the torment of the Cross. The Father did not send Jesus to Calvary. He went with Him. The Cross represents the spontaneous gift of unconditional love on the part of God: Father, Son, and Holy Spirit.

In the Eucharist we are given the Beloved Son on whom God's favor rests. This is the Beloved Son of the Baptism, the Transfiguration, and the Cross. If we truly realize what a powerful and life-giving action of love is given to us in the Eucharist, we would all be there every week. Participating in Mass on Sunday is not doing something for God though it is an opportunity for worship and praise. Participating in Sunday Mass allows God to do something wonderful for us.

Still, one of the reasons people stop going to Mass or stay away from Mass for a time is that they are angry at God because of something that happened that made them feel a victim of the Father rather than beloved of the Father. We make God into a puppeteer capriciously pulling the strings of human fate. We think God does bad things to good people to teach them a lesson or that God at least allows bad things to happen.

The Eucharist is God's answer to this false notion. The Eucharist is the continuation of Calvary where God in Jesus Christ gives Himself totally to us in order to be with us when we need Him the most. In the midst of misfortune we are not the victims of an arbitrary God. We are the beloved of God and God's favor continues to rest upon us just as it did upon Jesus. The Father does not send evil into our lives. The Father, the Son, and the Holy Spirit weep with us in our sorrows, celebrate with us in our joys, and support us with constant love. This is what both Calvary and the Eucharist are all about.

In praying this final Mystery of Light, we are reminded by the gift of the Eucharist not to pray in order to change God's perspective into ours but to allow God to change our perspective into His. The Rosary is an exercise in trust and surrender. As such it is destined to be a harvest of holiness.

Reflections on the Rosary as Prayer

MANY of our friends of other religious traditions know that the Rosary is a spiritual treasure for Catholics. In many countries like India where Christians represent a minority, people of other religious traditions see Catholics devoutly carrying the rosary and using it as a precious help to pray. There is also a tradition among Catholics to recite the Rosary at a cross or a shrine by the roadside or at a significant crossroad in a village, especially during the month of May. While the Catholics pray the Rosary, people of other religious traditions stand behind in silence and respect. At the end of the prayer there is a spontaneous sharing of refreshments, which are offered by the Catholic community.

Some years ago I accompanied Cardinal Francis Arinze on a goodwill visit to the Supreme Buddhist Patriarch of Thailand in Bangkok. Welcoming the Cardinal with warmth and affection, the Buddhist Patriarch put his hand in his pocket and removed a pouch in which there was a rosary. He said to the Cardinal: "The Pope gave me this rosary on the occasion of his visit to Thailand. We Buddhist monks are not allowed to keep any objects in our bedrooms. But I make an exception to that rule. I keep this rosary by my bed. It is very dear to me."

Among pilgrims who come to Rome there are also people of different religious traditions. They are friends of Catholics in their own countries. After visiting places, which are significant to Catholic tradition, these pilgrims, who belong to other religious traditions, go and buy rosaries to give to their Catholic friends. These are brought reverently to a General Audience of the Holy Father or in St. Peter's Square on Sunday when the Holy Father recites the traditional Angelus prayer with pilgrims. With the blessings of the Pope these rosaries are taken home and given as precious gifts to their Catholic neighbors and friends. I have often met Hindus and Sikhs from India and Buddhists from Japan who have inquired from me as to where they could buy rosaries. These pilgrims of other religious traditions know well that after visiting a holy place the best gift they can bring home to give to their Catholic friends and neighbors is a rosary, which is blessed by the Holy Father.

The ritual custom of praying with a chain of beads is common to many religious traditions. In Hindu, Buddhist, Muslim, and Sikh traditions particularly this practice is widely diffused. The Sanskrit word, origin of Pali and Punjabi words, for the chain of beads is *mala* or *japa-mala*. In the Hindu religious tradition sacred words or names of God are remembered in a silent or muttered repetition with the help of *mala*. In the Buddhist religious tradition the *mala* is used to overcome 108 sinful desires in order to reach the state of Nirvana. In the Sikh religious tradition *nama-simaran* may be done in community prayer or in private meditation with the help of beads. The Sikhs believe that the "repetition of God's Name expunges grief, pain and fear and produces happiness everlasting." The practice of carrying the chain of beads by Muslim believers is quite conspicuous. With its help a Muslim believer prays the ninety-nine names of Allah.

—*Msgr. Felix A. Machado*

Chapter 3

The Sorrowful Mysteries

THE Sorrowful Mysteries invite us to be companions of compassion with Jesus Christ. That is, in praying the Sorrowful Mysteries we have the opportunity to walk with Jesus as He suffers and dies out of love for us. In John's first epistle he says that love consists in this: *"not that we have loved God but that He loved us and sent His Son as expiation for our sins. Beloved, if God so loved us, we also must love one another"* (1 John 4:10-11).

Compassion means to suffer with, to be with another in their suffering and pain. Compassion is not pity. When we pity others we can remain at a safe distance from them. In compassion we stand in the world of another without platitudes or solutions. Rather, in compassion we become one with others as we walk with them on their journey. It is not easy to pray the Sorrowful Mysteries because it is not easy to simply walk with Christ as He suffers out of love for us. We are tempted to rescue ourselves by watering down the sufferings of Christ or to rescue Christ by trying to take His sufferings away. Or we are tempted to pity Christ and thus remain at a safe distance. It is difficult to allow Christ to be Christ and to do all that He does out of love for us. It is difficult for us to allow Christ to love us. We want His love, but we are also afraid of His love. We do not think we are worthy of it, and we are afraid of the demands it will place upon us. Such unconditional, unmerited love is disarming and frightening. And so in these Sorrowful Mysteries we turn to Mary in order to walk with Christ.

We can best nurture the virtue of compassion through the heart of Mary. Mary's heart is a mother's heart. Mary's heart is a contemplative heart. For years Mary had learned to ponder Jesus in her heart. We saw how Mary began storing things in her heart soon after the birth of Jesus and when He was lost in the temple. We saw how Mary nudged Jesus forward with a woman's intuition and a mother's wisdom at the wedding in Cana. Simeon predicted that a sword would pierce Mary's soul. That prophecy would now be fulfilled as Mary stood in the shadow of the cross. Through Mary we can walk with Christ in these Sorrowful Mysteries. With Mary we can pray these decades that bring alive the saving actions of Jesus Christ.

There are two levels on which we can pray these Sorrowful Mysteries. The first is to be present to Christ as companions of compassion. This means allowing Christ to suffer and die for us and to accept His love, which can be so overwhelming. The second level is to bring our suffering to Him, to unite our suffering with His suffering. In this way our suffering can be a path to the discovery of meaning and purpose. Jesus did not suffer to prove His love for us. Jesus suffered in order to love us and give us eternal life. Jesus did not suffer for the sake of suffering as if suffering has value in itself. It does not. Suffering has value as an act of love. Jesus suffered as expiation for our sins.

Throughout the hidden life of Christ in Nazareth and throughout His public ministry Mary was a silent and supportive presence to her Son. Through the heart of Mary may we be a silent and supportive presence to Jesus Christ in these Sorrowful Mysteries.

The First Sorrowful Mystery: The Agony in the Garden

Matthew 26:36-46

JESUS does not want to be alone in the anguish He experiences before His Passion begins. He seeks the silent, supportive presence of His friends. In the background, either nearby or holding Him in her heart at home, Mary is also there.

This scene in an olive grove from long ago is played out in our world and in our lives today. For those in hospitals and nursing homes, for the homebound and the disabled, for the unemployed and the grieving the anguish of Jesus in Gethsemane is played out over and over again. *"My soul is sorrowful even to death. Remain here and keep watch with me"* (Matthew 26:38).

"Would you stay with me before the operation? I'm scared."

"Would you go with me to the police when I report this abuse? I need your support to have the courage to tell the truth."

"Can I call you tomorrow when I get home from my appointment with the oncologist?"

Sometimes we are the companions who lend a silent, supportive presence.

Sometimes we are the one who cannot face life alone. We ask others for help.

We are asked to be with Jesus as He prays in an intimate and anxious way to His beloved Father: *"If it is possible, let this cup pass from me . . . "* (Matthew 26: 39). After the death of my parents I prayed for a time before the twelfth station where Jesus dies on the cross: "Lord, take away my pain so that I can be a free and loving disciple." A woman in my parish calls upon God in her own beautiful way when I invite petitions at Mass: "Dear God, please give us a cure for cancer. I know you can do it. It's time. Too many people are suffering and dying." Yes, she has cancer and it has recently returned. Her prayer is becoming more anguished just as Jesus' prayer in the Garden was so intense that He sweat blood.

We can pray this first decade of the Sorrowful Mysteries on the two levels mentioned above. On one level Jesus invites us to be with Him. It will require great courage to pray as a silent, supportive presence to Jesus. It will be painful for us and threatening to us. Like the disciples we can escape. They chose the escape of sleep. We can escape by simply repeating the Hail Marys without any thought of Jesus in the Garden. We can run away by protecting ourselves from any pain we encounter in ourselves, in Jesus, and in others. Or we can accept the invitation of Jesus to watch and pray, not just for a moment or when it is convenient but always and in every way.

To accept this invitation of Jesus we need Mary and we especially need Mary's heart. In cooperation with God's grace Mary had formed her heart around her Son. Everything He said, everything He did found a place in her heart. Mary knew the art of contemplation. She stored in her heart the joys and sorrows, the events and the mysteries that came with being the mother of the Holy One of God. Through Mary's heart we can watch with Christ and pray with Him.

The other level of response we can bring to Gethsemane contains all the petitions we yearn to have granted and all the questions we demand be given answers. All this needs to be brought to Jesus if we are to move beyond anger and fear. Again, it is not a matter of what we ask for, but of how we pray. All prayer is an exercise in faith and trust. Jesus is our guide. From the depths of His human soul He let the Father know that He did not want to suffer but He also placed Himself in the Father's hands. He entrusted Himself to the wisdom of the divine plan.

In praying the mystery of the Agony in the Garden the two levels of response to Jesus come together. By being with Christ in His anguished prayer we learn how to pray ourselves. Jesus teaches us by example. His struggle is our struggle. Our struggle becomes one with Jesus when we entrust ourselves to God the way Jesus did. When Jesus rose from His prayer He was resolute and strong. He was one with the Father. He united His spirit with the plan for our salvation. He was ready for what lay ahead. He was ready for Calvary and the cross.

Are you? Am I? For this we pray.

The Second Sorrowful Mystery: The Scourging at the Pillar
Matthew 27:26

THE Sorrowful Mysteries select key events in the Passion of Christ. A whole human drama surrounds these events especially the scourging and crowning. Judas betrays Christ. Peter denies Christ. The former commits suicide in despair; the latter becomes the rock on which the Church is built. Both men sin and sin gravely. When Judas realizes his sin of betrayal he sees no way out and is overwhelmed by his own evil. When Peter realizes his sin of denial, he weeps bitterly but he looks to Christ.

Acknowledging our sinfulness is an important starting point for spiritual growth in our increasingly secular world. Science offers us psychological excuses for our actions. Our culture tells us that we are self-sufficient and that this life is all that counts. We need a spiritual perspective to counter the cultural myths of our time.

When I think of Jesus being stripped of His garments and whipped with forty lashes of the soldier's weapon of torture, I am astonished by the length and depth of Christ's love for me and I am tempted to be like Judas. I am tempted to be overwhelmed by my own sinfulness. Only when I allow myself to be touched by the tremendous love of Jesus do I realize how serious my sinfulness is. I am not worthy of this love Jesus offers with such generosity. I do not deserve this love. Furthermore, my sinfulness makes no sense in light of such love. It is so easy to despair when I see how weak I am and how prone I am to commit the same sins. When Jesus was arrested the disciples ran away. Judas hanged himself. Peter said he did not know the man. They each had a fatal flaw and so do I.

Within my complex self I am each of these people. Stripped of all my rationalizations and of all the masks I place before the world, I am a sinner in need of the very love of Christ that frightens and overwhelms me. It makes me want to flee but where would I go? The difference between Judas and Peter is not that Jesus loved one more than the other. Jesus suffered and died for Judas as much as He suffered and died for Peter. The difference between them is not found in the gravity of their sin. Betrayal and denial are cut from the same dark cloth of evil. The difference between them is found in their response to the realization of their sinfulness and how evil they had been. Judas despairs because of his own evil before he can experience the saving moment of Calvary and the cross. Peter weeps bitterly but doesn't flee. Albeit from a distance, a safe distance at that, Peter keeps looking to Christ.

Important as recognizing my sinfulness is, it is not enough in order to grow in the spiritual life. In itself, just recognizing my sinfulness can lead to despair as it did for Judas. I also need to recognize my need for redemption and I need to recognize the truth that redemption lies outside myself. I am not my own savior. Jesus is my Savior. Jesus is my hope.

Thus in the Sorrowful Mysteries we look to Christ. Everything that Jesus does He does out of love for you and me. Eventually this meant conversion on the part of Peter and the other disciples. Our appreciation of the suffering of Jesus can lead to our conversion. We too can turn away from sin and be faithful to the Gospel when we allow ourselves to deeply and personally feel the suffering of Christ and the love He so fully gives. This is a courageous way to pray the Sorrowful Mysteries, especially the scourging at the pillar. This is the way St. Francis of Assisi prayed the Passion of Christ.

> *"My Lord Jesus Christ, I pray you to grant me two graces before I die: the first is that during my life I may feel in my soul and in my body, as much as possible, that pain which You, dear Jesus, sustained in the hour of Your most bitter Passion. The second is that I may feel in my heart, as much as possible, that excessive love with which You, O Son of God, were inflamed in willingly enduring such suffering for us sinners"* (Little Flowers of Francis, Third Consideration).

Notice that twice Francis says "as much as possible." It is important to remember two things as you pray these Sorrowful Mysteries: pray as you can, not as you can't, and do not try to run faster than grace.

As we pray the Second Sorrowful Mystery we bond ourselves to Mary who prayed while Jesus was being whipped in Pilate's courtyard. She remained faithful to the grace God gave her. By divine mercy Mary was spared the pain of witnessing the scene. But she knew her Son was in danger and was being tortured according to the cruelty of the time. Once again, it is Mary who can lead us to Christ. By joining our heart to her heart, we seek union with Christ in this second Sorrowful Mystery.

The Third Sorrowful Mystery: The Crowning with Thorns

Matthew 27:27-31

The suffering endured by Jesus in His Passion due to physical torture is repugnant for us. This suffering is clear evidence of love.

But there is an even greater suffering endured by Jesus that is further evidence of His unconditional love for us. The psychological and emotional suffering of Jesus is beyond our ability to comprehend. Jesus was truly God and truly man. He was like us in all things but sin. His divinity did not protect Him from his humanity, save sin. He assumed the burden of our humanity so that He could heal our humanity of sin and instill into our hearts the marvelous love of our Creator. *"He emptied Himself, taking the form of a slave, coming in human likeness; and found human in appearance, He humbled Himself, becoming obedient to death, even death on a cross"* (Philippians 2:7-8).

In the crowning with thorns we are invited to be present to the person of Christ, for in this Sorrowful Mystery Jesus is humiliated. He is humiliated by several physical actions. He is stripped naked. He is covered with a military cloak. His head is pierced with a makeshift crown and a reed is stuck in his right hand. Then He is humiliated by those who surround Him as they make a mockery of who He is.

How must Jesus have felt at this time? How alone He was, abandoned by His friends, ridiculed by His enemies. This is Jesus, the Holy One of God, the Son of God sent for our salvation. When we feel humiliated and abandoned, we feel alone and tend to feel sorry for ourselves and angry at the world. We think that God has forgotten us and is punishing us. All too often we blame God for our misfortune. Tragically, we turn away from God just when we need God the most. Jesus suffered the very depths of human misery not only so that He could redeem us but also in order to be with us when we truly need Him.

For us to move beyond the anger and resentment we accumulate when life is cruel, we might return to the two levels of presence to Jesus mentioned earlier. The first level involves our silent, supportive presence to Christ humiliated and abandoned. The second level is to bring into conversation with the weak and humble Christ our own psychological and emotional vulnerability, and from the depths of our wounded souls, to cry out to the Son of the living God.

◯◡◯

In praying this third Sorrowful Mystery we are presented with a new opportunity: not simply to appreciate what Jesus did for us in His Passion but also to appreciate what Jesus experienced as a real flesh and blood person in His Passion. Admittedly, this is very hard to do. But I heartily recommend that you pray in this way in order to draw closer to Christ.

Both the physical suffering of Jesus and the humiliation He endured as a person are attempts by Christ to be one with us as we bear our human burden. In praying this third Sorrowful Mystery we can best pray from our weakness the way St. Paul did in Corinthians.

St. Paul rejoiced in his weakness because he discovered that when he was weak, then he was strong. He asked God to remove some human failing but God kept him humble, telling Paul: *"My grace is sufficient for you, for power is made perfect in weakness"* (2 Corinthians 12:9).

Jesus gives us an enlightening example of this when He is crowned with thorns. He seems so weak and so helpless in the face of ridicule. And yet He is so powerful in His passion and death that all of humanity is saved from sin.

St. Paul actually boasted of his weakness so that the power of Christ might dwell with him. *"Therefore, I am content with weaknesses, insults, hardships, persecutions, and constraints, for the sake of Christ; for when I am weak, then I am strong"* (2 Corinthians 12:10).

This is not for the fainthearted but, then again, the Rosary is a very powerful prayer.

The Fourth Sorrowful Mystery: Jesus Carries the Cross
Luke 23:26-32

W*E adore You, O Christ and we praise You;
for by Your Holy Cross You have redeemed the world.*

Much pent up anger has spilled into the streets of Israel, Afghanistan, and Iraq in recent times. We have seen on television how disorderly and frightening an angry mob can be. This gives us some sense of what it was like when Jesus carried His cross to Golgotha. The people are in a frenzy and Jesus is the object of their anger. This scene is chaotic and confusing. The pumped up crowd of people who demanded Jesus be crucified roar their way to Calvary.

Simon of Cyrene is a companion of compassion to Jesus by the merciful act of carrying the heavy cross. By all accounts he doesn't do so willingly. He happens to pass by and is pressed into service. He doesn't know Jesus and could presume from the jeering crowd that this man is a criminal.

We can best pray this fourth Sorrowful Mystery by being Simon. We know nothing about him but we can give flesh to his anonymity by the content of our own lives. At this point in the journey we can be a companion of compassion to Christ by bearing the cross, both His and ours.

If the truth were told, we may not want to carry the cross any more than Simon does. We too are often asked to carry a cross we do not want. An aging parent may be a real cross even though we hate to admit that he or she is a burden. A child who becomes estranged from us due to addiction or to some bad decisions becomes a painful cross on a parent's heart. Illness and unemployment inter-rupt our lives and weigh us down.

When we carry these crosses with a continuing faith in Jesus Christ, we become Simon on the way to Calvary. Jesus did not just carry a wooden cross to Calvary. Jesus carried the burden of humanity to Calvary. Jesus carried all our crosses to Calvary, the ones we carried yesterday and the ones we will carry tomorrow. There is no separa-tion between the cross of Christ and the crosses we bear. Jesus suffered and died in order to be one with us when we need Him the most.

Questions concerning suffering and evil have become poignant since September 11th. Where was God on September 11th? Did He save some people but let other people die? Did he allow it to happen or could He have intervened? These are difficult questions and they arise from the searing pain in people's hearts, not from the dis-tance of an intellectual quest. In the face of such massive evil, some people turn away from God, unable to reconcile a loving God with such unspeakable evil. I believe that God's one overwhelming desire is that each one of us be saved and be united with Him forever in Heaven. Therefore, I believe that God was with each person on September 11th. I believe Jesus wept with those who died and rejoiced with those who escaped.

I do not believe that God is a puppeteer manipulat-ing the events of our lives or a master teacher trying to teach us lessons by sending us pain. One of the implica-tions of evil is that this life is fragile and arbitrary. It is tem-porary and limited. Only in God will our souls be at rest. (cf. Psalm 62). Only in God will we find true joy and last-ing peace.

Before we finish praying this fourth Sorrowful Mystery we might pray with Mary. In the midst of the swirling crowd we will find Mary and some of her family, all women of faithfulness and courage. Surely Mary's heart was one with the heart of Jesus on the way to Calvary. Her sufferings are one with the sufferings of her Son. And so she is a better example for us than Simon. He was a reluctant helper. Mary is a silent, supportive lover. Let us find in Mary the strength to walk with Christ. Her presence on the way of the cross lifted up the tired spirit of Jesus. I imagine their eyes meeting as He fell a third time. Through eyes streaming with tears, Mary encouraged Jesus to be faithful to His Father's affairs. Together they mounted the hill of Golgotha. Nails pierced the hands and feet of Christ. A sword pierced the soul of Mary, His Mother.

We adore You, O Christ, and we praise You;
For by Your Holy Cross You have redeemed the world.

The Fifth Sorrowful Mystery: Jesus Dies on the Cross
Matthew 27:46-50; John 19:25-30

THE crowds have left by now; the disciples have run away. Only a few soldiers and some women remain. The crowds lost interest once Jesus was raised on the cross. The disciples had long since left the company of the suffering Christ. They had stopped walking with Him in the Garden of Gethsemane when they refused to accept a very real part of Jesus, namely, His willingness to follow the divine plan of salvation.

This fifth Sorrowful Mystery is best prayed on our knees or in some humble posture that marks this extraordinary moment. And it is best prayed in hope because Jesus gives gifts of life as He hangs upon the cross. First, He gives life through forgiveness. In the midst of His agony He speaks to His beloved Father: *"Father, forgive them for they know not what they do"* (Luke 23:34). The death of Christ on the cross brings us forgiveness of our sins. All we need do is simply turn to Christ and truly repent of our sins. The first gift Jesus gives on the cross is the gift of forgiveness. We are not our own saviors. Jesus is our Savior. Our salvation lies outside ourselves and is found here on earth when Jesus dies on the cross. Praying the Rosary should motivate us to confess our sins.

The second gift we are given is the gift of trust. Jesus expresses His trust in the Father's love twice on the cross. The first time he cries out: *"My God, my God, why have You abandoned Me?"* (Matthew 27:46). This sounds like anything but an expression of trust but Jesus is quoting Psalm 22, which begins in despair and ends in trust. When we pray it is important that we pray from the depths of our souls, not from some polite place we think is acceptable to God. *"Out of the depths I cry to You, Lord; Lord, hear my cry! May your ears be attentive to my cry for mercy"* (Psalm 130:1-2).

The scandal of the cross is precisely the truth that Jesus brings life out of death, hope out of despair. This final Sorrowful Mystery abounds with life and hope. On Calvary Jesus explodes with love upon the earth. And then He entrusts Himself totally to the Father: *"Father, into Your hands I commend my spirit"* (Luke 23:46).

Our confidence is not in ourselves. Our confidence is in Jesus Christ. In this fifth Sorrowful Mystery we pray with trust as we entrust those we love and ourselves to God. All prayer is an exercise in faith and trust.

The third gift of life given on Calvary is found in John's Gospel. Jesus commends Mary to John and John to Mary. He asks His beloved disciple to care for His Mother. *"And from that hour the disciple took her into his home"* (John 19:27). A new relationship is born at the foot of the cross. It is a relationship characterized by mutual respect and care. It is Jesus' final gift to us: the gift of relationships that are founded and supported in Jesus Christ.

We are all equal at the foot of the cross. We are all beloved in the shadow of the cross. And yet, we all know how hard it is to love everyone equally and totally. Some people are easier to love than others. Some people seem impossible to love. Others may need tough love in order to grow. In the real world where we live each day, love is a challenge, to say the least.

In praying this final Sorrowful Mystery we should avoid the temptation to idealize or spiritualize the challenges of love. To put it simply, life is difficult and love is often beyond our grasp. Left to us it may seem, and at times be, impossible. This is precisely why we need Jesus Christ to die on the cross for us. We know from the beginning of the story of Christ at the Annunciation that nothing is impossible with God.

And so, in the shadow of the cross we seek life and our own redemption. Being loved so unconditionally and so completely, we can now love one another but only in, with, and through Jesus Christ. We might stand with Mary in the shadow of the cross. A sword pierced her soul when they placed the body of her Son in her arms. Still, her faith and trust remained steadfast.

Forgiveness, trust, and new relationships are the three gifts Jesus gives us on Calvary. Our task is to accept these gifts and then give them away. We have a good beginning of this when we pray the Rosary for peace in the world, for our enemies and our friends, and for those most in need. The Rosary then provides a good beginning for the challenges of love. If we can love others by praying for them we might love them when we meet them. Mary will show us the way and Jesus will give us the grace.

Reflections on the Rosary
as Prayer

I FIND that my Rosary is a "comfort zone" like "comfort food" to some. When I reach for my beads I start to feel warmed by the familiar zone that praying the Rosary gives me. When I was a young girl and would be nervous or upset or scared or whatever it was that I cried to my mother about, she would offer words of encouragement, ending with "and reach into your pocket and hold your rosary beads. The Blessed Mother is always with you." That gave me such comfort and confidence. This helped me to survive countless brushes with disaster (in my mind).

Somewhere along my path in life, I lost touch with my beads. I thought I had gained enough confidence to go it on my own. When I had children I often prayed to the Blessed Mother to open her sweet motherly arms and embrace my children, love them as I do, remove their fears, and hold them in her arms out of harm's way.

When my children started going out at night, I was so worried about them, I couldn't relax, much less sleep. On a trip to Ireland, I picked up a bunch of those 'Irish Worry-Stones' as gifts for people at home. I thought I could lie in bed and be comforted by the smooth, cool stone created for the intention of being worried upon. Then, as if I had done it every night for years, I reached for my rosary beads. And there I was, back in the arms of the Blessed Mother. Now I felt Mary really understood my fears; now, I too was a mother.

I pray the Rosary often these days. I ask Mary, the Mother of Jesus, to help my children to have confidence in themselves. When my daughter reveals her fears to me, I ask her if she has her rosary beads in her pocket.

—*Denise Kretz*

MARY is a model of faith. She is gentle yet strong. She is compassionate yet powerful. She is the model of a woman of faith. She is the woman in whose likeness I would like to grow.

When one looks at the life of Mary as portrayed in the writings and traditions of our Church, she emulates goodness and kindness. As a young, innocent girl she is asked to bear the child of God. This would be a life-changing event that could cause her much pain, embarrassment and banishment from the community. She understood this and said "yes" in spite of all. She is courageous.

After carrying her child in her womb for nine months and delivering him in the most humble surroundings, she comes to find her infant son's life is in danger. Yet, she obeys the direction given to her and never loses sight of the One who will protect her and her family from harm. She is obedient.

These are some of the traits I have come to respect and honor in Mary. I was not raised with any particular devotion to Mary. I knew her as the Mother of God. I prayed the Hail Mary. I remember many different statues of a woman fully clothed in long dresses. My elementary school was named after her holy name. This would sum up my connection to Mary throughout most of my life.

I understand now that many people prayed to Mary to bring their petitions to the Father. I went straight to the

Source. I never knew any different. I was a fearless kid who never had any major concerns. Yet I was always in relationship with God. I see that now in hindsight.

As a woman, I have grown quite fond of Mary, Mother of God. She is the source of much wisdom, strength and faith. I look to her to guide me now. I look to her as a model of faith when mine seems to be failing. I look to her as a model of strength when the world, my Church or my family overburdens me and I feel deflated. I look to her for wisdom because I only seem to have more questions, never any answers.

Mary's life, like Jesus' life, was centered on prayer. Both came to know the will of God through prayer, through nourishing their relationship with their Creator. This has been a hard lesson for me. Prayer is essential if I want to come to know and do the will of God. I am a woman of action. I need to be more a woman of prayer, of silence, of solitude. I need to let God in and allow time to hear God's gentle calling, God's quiet urging.

Praying the Rosary is exactly the tool I need. It quiets me down. It centers me. It focuses me. Praying the Rosary encourages me. It is the tool I need to be obedient to the will of God. Praying the Rosary can't be done quickly. This is a good lesson for me, an impatient, impetuous person. The Rosary allows me to turn down the noise and be alone with God.

Mary is a model of faith. She is wise, gentle and strong. The Rosary is a great vehicle to help me grow closer to God and to be more like Mary who is courageous, obedient and faithful and who emulates goodness and kindness. *—Tricia Callahan*

Chapter 4

The Glorious Mysteries

A GREAT shift both in emotion and in faith takes place when we pray the Glorious Mysteries. In the Sorrowful Mysteries we journeyed with Jesus as He suffered and died for us. With the Glorious Mysteries we enter a whole new realm of faith. Now we celebrate the magnificent vision God sets before us. We celebrate the Kingdom of Heaven where Jesus lives and reigns with the Father and the Holy Spirit. We celebrate the coming of the Holy Spirit upon the apostles and upon us. And we celebrate the unique place of Mary in the Kingdom of Heaven.

Jesus conquers evil when He dies on the cross. Jesus overcomes death when He rises on the third day. The Glorious Mysteries proclaim the power of God and the love of God. The Glorious Mysteries proclaim that the power of God's love is greater than the power of evil. The Glorious Mysteries proclaim that life prevails over death.

"If for this life only we have hoped in Christ we are the most pitiable people of all" (1 Corinthians 15:19). A whole new vision opens before us when we pray the Glorious Mysteries. Jesus rises from the dead and ascends to His Father in Heaven. The Holy Spirit inspires the disciples to become apostles. Mary takes her place in the community of God, preserved for all eternity, body and soul, as the beautiful person she was on earth.

Let us pray these Glorious Mysteries with confidence in God. Let us ask God to deepen our faith as we ponder these powerful truths.

The First Glorious Mystery: Jesus Rises from the Dead
Luke 24:1-12

IN July 2002 we lived through an intense drama when nine miners were trapped underground. It seemed an eternity as rescuers tried to reach the men. What an exhilarating experience it was not only for them and their families but also for the entire nation when each man was hoisted to safety. I can still remember the joy of the announcement that all nine were alive. We called it a miracle and indeed it was. It remains in my memory as an experience of resurrection.

I am Irish enough to believe that if life goes well for an extended time, something will happen to spoil the joy. I am also Irish enough to think that if I receive a blessing I'll pay for it in some way down the road. I laugh at myself when I react this way. I have learned to appreciate life and enjoy life as I have gotten older and have experienced other ethnic groups who approach life differently. Living in Italy is a good antidote to growing up Irish!

There is no down side to the Resurrection of Christ. That Easter morning was an experience of pure joy. *"Why do you seek the living one among the dead? He is not here, but He has been raised"* (Luke 24:5b-6). The first reaction to the Resurrection was surprise and disbelief. They were not prepared for the Resurrection because they did not participate in the Crucifixion. They would have to go back and remember everything that Jesus said and did in order to appreciate the astounding event before them. Peter would have to admit his denial; the others would have to face their fear. Even then it would only be with the gift of the

Holy Spirit that they would receive the insight and courage they needed to preach and live the message of Jesus Christ.

What do you need in order to pray this first Glorious Mystery with faith? The only way to the Resurrection is through the Crucifixion. The only way to appreciate life is to experience death. The best way to pray this first Glorious Mystery is with open hands and a surrendering heart. In this way we can receive the gift of life the Resurrection offers us. If our hands are tightened in a fist because we are clinging to this life with insecurity and fear, we will not be able to accept the gift of the Resurrection. If our hearts are closed because we have been hurt and will not allow ourselves to be hurt again, we will not experience the joy that the Risen Christ brings to us. Regrets from the past and fear of the future can be real obstacles to us when we pray this Glorious Mystery.

Did you hear the commercial about the woman who is afraid of losing her money in the stock market? She ends her conversation with her friend by saying: "I just don't know what to do with my money." Unrealistic as this may sound, a good response to a culture of possessions is: "Give it away." How free we would be if we could do this. We can better appreciate the Resurrection if we love passionately but with a gentle grasp on life.

Another commercial involves a husband and wife who can't decide which expensive car to buy. The wife proclaims their solution: "So we bought them both." How sad from a perspective of faith and care for the poor. Our culture says that the one who dies with the most toys wins. I think that the one who dies with the most toys loses.

When we pray with faith we are saying that this life is not the total experience of life. We are saying that this life is only a preparation for a life with God beyond our imagining. When Jesus rose from the dead He conquered death not only in His own life but also for all of human life. He created a path for us to live with Him forever and He went to prepare that experience for us.

"Why look among the dead for someone who is alive?" (Luke 24:5). As we pray the first Glorious Mystery, the angel's question to the women on Easter morning is worthy of our prayer today. We look among the dead for someone who is alive when we cling to our possessions and to one another. We will find life when we love freely and gently. We look among the dead for someone who is alive when we isolate ourselves for fear of being hurt. We will find life when we take risks in love the way Jesus and Mary did. We look among the dead for someone who is alive when we take drugs or abuse alcohol in search of happiness. We will find life when we surrender ourselves to God's love.

Jesus is alive. He is risen from the dead. Jesus is our salvation and our hope. In Him we live and move and have our being.

The Second Glorious Mystery: Jesus Ascends into Heaven

Acts 1:9-11

WHEN I was in high school I worked in a camp and became friends with a counselor a few years older than I. At the end of the second summer he was sent to Rome to study for the priesthood. In those days they traveled by boat. There is something very dramatic about a ship leaving shore. After the initial goodbye, I searched to find him on the deck. This led to waving goodbye until my friend was out of sight. It was one of my first experiences in saying goodbye and I felt it deeply. The emptiness was tangible and took some time to pass.

Years later when I went to Rome to work there, I left by plane and just disappeared through the gate, hardly as dramatic as a ship leaving shore. This first-time leaving drew a host of friends. Good friends brought their three little boys. Everyone left the airport except my friends and their sons. The Kretz boys would not leave until they saw "Jimmy Mac's" plane leave. After what seemed an eternity the parents picked out a plane and proclaimed my departure. They described the drive home in terms similar to my experience with the ship years before. Something special had ended; something new had yet to begin.

I do not like goodbyes and don't do them terribly well. When I am leaving I would rather disappear through the gate than have the long goodbyes of the ship. When friends are leaving I am keenly aware that life is changing and will never be the same again. I can remember the same friends mentioned above speaking of the last summer before the boys went to school and how they wanted to enjoy that special time before life changed.

There are inevitable losses in life, precious moments in relationships and precious relationships that are not repeatable. The men and women who formed the company of Jesus experience this kind of loss and emptiness when He ascends into heaven. He tells them the Holy Spirit will come upon them and that He will always be with them, but they sense it will not be the same. They stand there paralyzed on life's journey as they gaze up at the sky.

My father died suddenly a month before I left for Rome. My mother had died some years before and so I found myself at a crossroads. My life had changed dramatically and would never be the same again. At thirty-seven I still had much before me, living in a foreign country and beginning a new job. But, before I could step into the future I had to come to terms with the past. I had to mourn the losses before I could embrace what lie ahead.

The ascension of Jesus provides each of us the opportunity to grow in faith. As we get older it is easy for us to look back to the good old days when life seemed simpler and God seemed closer. The inevitable losses we endure along the way take a toll on us. We can become resentful and bitter. When this happens our lives become smaller and our enthusiasm for life diminishes.

As the disciples gazed up into the sky they had no idea what lie ahead. They were paralyzed in the present moment. They were soon to discover that Jesus had not abandoned them. As a matter of fact, Jesus had much in store for them through the gift of the Holy Spirit. They discovered that the best was yet to come.

As you pray this second Glorious Mystery, you might need to place into the hands of the Risen Christ all the resentment and bitterness that have accumulated in your heart. You may have to revisit the past before you can live in hope in the present. This may involve mourning the loss of loved ones, letting go of old hurts and disappointments, forgiving yourself for your failures and forgiving others for their sins.

This might be a good time to visit with Mary again. Remember how she stored things in her heart and pondered them. Surely Mary was there when Jesus ascended into heaven. I think she was there in a different way than the others. They were shocked and disappointed. They felt Jesus had abandoned them. But Mary knew that Jesus had to leave. She had learned to let Him go when He was twelve years old. She knew she would be fine and that Jesus had more to give them than they could receive at that time.

Mary is a good companion for our prayer in this second Glorious Mystery. She can lead us to Christ. She can teach us to hope. She can help us prepare to receive the gifts that are yet to come.

The Third Glorious Mystery: The Holy Spirit Descends upon the Apostles
Acts 2:1-4

THIS is a beautiful Mystery to pray. In this prayer we affirm our belief that all is gift, all is grace. We are dependent upon God for our very life and we are dependent upon God for the gifts of person and personality that form our ability to love.

This dependence is not weakness; it is confidence because God is not arbitrary with His gifts. He gives the gifts freely and wisely. Furthermore, God does not withdraw His gifts. They are irrevocable. The disciples needed the gifts of insight and courage in order to live the Christian life. What are the gifts you need at this time in your life? We often pray for the needs of others and this is certainly a good way to pray. I pray the Rosary every Thursday for one friend and every Friday for another friend. They know I am doing this and they feel supported by it.

I think it is also valuable to pray for ourselves and this third Glorious Mystery provides us the opportunity to ask God for the gifts we need at this time in our lives. It is not selfish to pray for ourselves because we are asking for gifts that we can share with others. The coming of the Holy Spirit is an opportunity for us to take a new look at ourselves as loved by God.

After the experience of the Jubilee Year that inaugurated this new millennium, Pope John Paul II invited us to start afresh from Christ. It is in this spirit of newness and discovery that we can best pray this third Glorious

Mystery. We can easily become discouraged when we encounter the same faults in ourselves and when we face the same challenges year after year. There is a routine to life that can drain our energy and diminish our enthusiasm. With the gift of the Spirit, we can start afresh from Christ. In praying this third Glorious Mystery we might pray with new ears that are open to what God has to say and with new eyes that are anxious to see what God is doing here and now in our lives. We have been told (Matthew 7:7) to ask and it will be given to us, to seek and we shall find. In praying over the gift of the Spirit, let us ask openly for what we need to live the Christian life today.

We might pray for the gift of peace. The Holy Father has suggested that we pray the Rosary for peace in the world today, especially since the terrorists' attacks of September 11th. We can start afresh from Christ by praying for peace in our own hearts and in our world. Jesus is our peace.

We might pray for the gift of hope. Our world and our Church are in tremendous turmoil. There is much discouragement and disillusionment amongst people of faith. At the conclusion of his Apostolic Letter, *Novo Millennio Ineunte,* Pope John Paul II urged us to go forward in hope: "A new millennium is opening before the Church like a vast ocean upon which we shall venture, relying on the help of Christ. The Son of God, who became incarnate two thousand years ago out of love for humanity, is at work even today: we need discerning eyes to see this and, above all, a generous heart to become the instruments of His work." In these most difficult of times we need to start afresh from Christ and stay close to Him so that we might move forward together in hope. Jesus is our hope.

Finally in praying this mystery, let us pray for the gift of perseverance. In all of Scripture Mary is the model and the inspiration for the gift of perseverance. I often ask people as a penance to say the Hail Mary and to ask Mary for the gift of perseverance. Throughout her life, from the time the angel announced her special role in salvation to the moment in Pentecost when she received the Holy Spirit, Mary persevered in faithfulness to the present moment. As we turn to Mary in these last Glorious Mysteries, let us ask her to intercede for us with the gift of perseverance. When all the recent scandals in the Church were raging in the press a woman came out of Mass and said: "I guess you just have to keep on keeping on." How right she was and how difficult it has been to persevere.

Hail Mary, full of grace, help me to persevere through these trying times. *The Lord is with thee.* Help me to remain enthusiastic for Christ and the Church in the face of greater challenges. *Blessed art thou among women and blessed is the fruit of your womb, Jesus.* Help me to keep my eyes fixed firmly on Christ in the midst of this stormy sea. *Holy Mary, Mother of God, pray for us sinners, now and at the hour of our death. Amen.*

The Fourth Glorious Mystery: Mary is Assumed into Heaven

MARY has been our companion throughout the Gospel-based Mysteries of the Rosary. She was the first disciple of her Son. She began to be in His company when she said yes to Gabriel's announcement.

Mary was in the forefront of the Joyful Mysteries where she played such a vital role in the birth and the hidden life of Christ. She was in the background during the ministry of Christ and His Passion as we have seen in the Luminous and Sorrowful Mysteries. And yet her presence and influence were evident. We pray these Mysteries with her silent, supportive presence to her Son and to us.

In these Glorious Mysteries we also experience Mary's presence as we join her in rejoicing at the Resurrection of Christ and the gift of the Holy Spirit. The last two Glorious Mysteries honor Mary for the unique role she played in the unfolding plan of our salvation and for the example of faithfulness and trust she has given us.

Of all the memorable places in our beautiful world, my favorite place is Assisi, the medieval city of St. Francis and St. Clare. I wrote these reflections while on vacation in Assisi during the summer of 2003. When I am in Assisi I feel very much at home. If I am there for a couple of weeks, I especially like arriving that first day. The sisters at the guesthouse are always very welcoming. They are like family during my stay. When I turn the key to my room, I have an overwhelming feeling of arrival. I am home and this brings me peace.

The Assumption of Mary into heaven is her experience of arriving home. Jesus welcomed her into the community He shares for all eternity with the Father and the Holy Spirit. Never would there be a more gracious welcome. Never would there be more joy than this moment when the handmaid of the Lord arrived home. All the mysteries and events Mary had stored in her heart were now surrendered to God and replaced with the peace only her Son could give.

Have you had the experience of arriving somewhere and feeling you were finally home? For some people this experience is a place, like Assisi is for me. For other people it is an experience. I have heard people describe this feeling when they walked into a Church after years of searching or when they walked into an AA meeting after years of struggling.

And yet, even though we may feel we have finally come home, we are still on a journey. Our experience of feeling at home here in this transient world is but a preamble for what God has in store for us. On some level Mary might have felt she arrived at home whenever she, Joseph, and Jesus returned to Nazareth after their annual pilgrimage to Jerusalem. But this probably felt less than home after Joseph died and Jesus left. Or perhaps she felt she finally arrived at home when her dying Son commended her to John and the evangelist took her into his home.

I think that because Mary lived such a contemplative life, because she pondered in her heart what she did not understand, because she lived in appreciation of her Son, she knew in her heart both at Nazareth and in John's house that she was not yet home. I think Mary realized she was home when she was assumed into heaven.

The best way to pray the fourth Glorious Mystery is to appreciate that Mary has arrived home and to recognize that we have not yet arrived home. Hopefully we all have experiences of feeling at home whether it be with family or with friends, in a place that is familiar or while visiting a distant land. We should enjoy feeling at home but we should not settle there. Yes, the best is yet to come. This is why those who die with the most toys lose. They think they have everything they need and they fight to hold on to it and protect it. But we have here no lasting city. We are not yet home.

The Fifth Glorious Mystery: Mary is Crowned Queen of Heaven and Earth

MARY continues to play a key role in the unfolding of God's plan for our salvation. "In a wholly singular way she cooperated by her obedience, faith, hope, and burning charity in the Savior's work of restoring supernatural life to souls. For this reason she is a mother to us in the order of grace" (*Lumen Gentium* 53:63).

These words from the Second Vatican Council express well the place that Mary can play in our Christian living today. Mary now enjoys the life of resurrection Jesus promised. She is completely united with her Son in the community of the love of the Father, the Son, and the Holy Spirit whom we worship as God. Since the Council of Ephesus in 431 the Church has proclaimed Mary as the Mother of God. This title honors Mary for her unique role of trust and faith that enabled her to cooperate with God's plan. Her dignity as a woman of faith is unique in our Christian history.

As mother of God, Mary is also mother of the Church, which is the sacramental presence of Jesus in the world today. Furthermore, Mary is our mother in the order of grace. It is most appropriate for us to turn to Mary and ask her intercession. She is for us a model of faith and trust, and she is an inspiration for us who seek to follow Jesus closely. As the mother of God, Mary bore Jesus into our world. As Queen of heaven and earth, Mary is the bearer of grace for each of us.

The joy of praying the Rosary is the Christian joy of seeking union with Jesus through Mary. The Rosary is centered on the life, death, and resurrection of Jesus Christ. As John the Evangelist tells us with characteristic directness: *"Yes, God so loved the world that He gave us His only Son so that everyone who believes in Him may not be lost but may have eternal life"* (John 3:16). God has chosen us because He loves us. It is God's deep desire that each of us live in union with Him forever in heaven. This is the source of our joy as Christian men and women.

Through Mary God reached out to us by becoming one of us. Through Mary we can accept God's love by imitating her trust and faith. Through praying the Rosary we can ponder with Mary the mysteries of love expressed and lived in Jesus Christ. With Mary, the first disciple, we seek Christ. With Mary, the first apostle, we can find Christ. With Mary, the first pilgrim, we will appreciate Christ, the Son of the living God. The joy of praying the Rosary is similar to the joy Mary experienced when she visited Elizabeth. Like Mary we can say: *"My soul proclaims the greatness of the Lord, my spirit rejoices in God my Savior"* (Luke 1:46).

❧

In this Glorious Mystery we can pray to the Queen of heaven and earth and ask her to keep us on the path that leads us home. Once again Mary shows us the way to her Son. As we pray this Mystery that celebrates Mary's special place in the Kingdom of heaven, let us ask Mary's intercession so that we can be true pilgrims in this land. Mary was not only the first disciple of Christ. She was also the first pilgrim of faith. The best way to pray the Rosary is to pray as a pilgrim. A pilgrim enjoys the present moment. A pilgrim appreciates the beauty of a place. A pilgrim rejoices in the gift of life. But a pilgrim knows he or she is on a journey and is not yet home. A pilgrim knows that the best is yet to come.

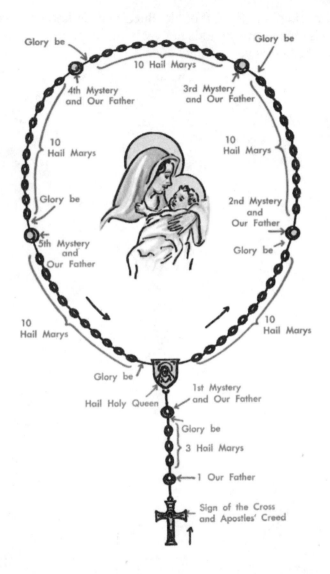

Glory be

Glory be

10 Hail Marys

4th Mystery
and Our Father

3rd Mystery
and Our Father

10
Hail Marys

10
Hail Marys

Glory be

2nd Mystery
and
Our Father

5th Mystery
and
Our Father

Glory be

10
Hail Marys

10
Hail Marys

Glory be

1st Mystery
and Our Father

Hail Holy Queen

Glory be

3 Hail Marys

1 Our Father

Sign of the Cross
and Apostles' Creed

OTHER OUTSTANDING CATHOLIC BOOKS

HOLY BIBLE—St. Joseph Edition of the completely modern translation called the New American Bible. Large type with helpful Notes and Maps, Photographs, Family Record and Bible Dictionary. 1600 pages.

Ask for No. 611

St. Joseph SUNDAY MISSAL—Complete Edition. All **3 cycles A, B, and C** with all Mass texts, illustrations, Prayers and Devotions. 1600 pages.

Ask for No. 820

IMITATION OF CHRIST—By Thomas A Kempis. New edition. The one book that is second only to the Bible in popularity. Large type, illustrated.

Ask for No. 320

MINUTE MEDITATIONS FOR EACH DAY—By Rev. Bede Naegele, O.C.D. Short Scripture text, reflection, and prayer for each day that can be read in two minutes. 365 illustrations in color. **Ask for No. 190**

POPE JOHN PAUL II AND THE LUMINOUS MYSTERIES OF THE ROSARY—By Rev. Jerome M. Vereb, C.P. An invaluable look at some of the reasons why Pope John Paul II added the Luminous Mysteries to the Rosary that provides a clear presentation of the biblical truths in which those mysteries are rooted.

Ask for No. 118

DICTIONARY OF MARY—A valuable book that is equal to a short summa about the Blessed Virgin. Written by foremost scholars, it sets forth in quick dictionary form the most important Catholic teachings about Mary.

Ask for No. 367

PRAY THE ROSARY—The most popular, handy, purse-size Rosary booklet. Each Mystery, including the new Luminous Mysteries, is gloriously illustrated in full color with appropriate text. **Ask for No. 40**

CATHOLIC BOOK OF PRAYERS—By Rev. Maurus FitzGerald. Today's most popular general prayerbook, printed in Giant Type. Contains many favorite prayers—for Everyday, to the Blessed Trinity, to Mary, and the Saints.

Ask for No. 910

IMITATION OF MARY—By Rev. Alexander de Rouville, S.J. New modern version of the Companion Volume to the "Imitation of Christ." The author follows Mary through the different mysteries and circumstances of her life.

Ask for No. 330

MARY DAY BY DAY—Minute meditations for every day of the year including: (1) a Scripture passage; (2) a quotation from the Saints; and (3) a concluding prayer. Printed in two colors with over 300 illustrations.

Ask for No. 180

WHEREVER CATHOLIC BOOKS ARE SOLD

Additional Titles Published by Resurrection Press, a Catholic Book Publishing Imprint

A Rachel Rosary *Larry Kupferman*	$4.50
Blessings All Around *Dolores Leckey*	$8.95
Catholic Is Wonderful *Mitch Finley*	$4.95
Come, Celebrate Jesus! *Francis X. Gaeta*	$4.95
Days of Intense Emotion *Keeler/Moses*	$12.95
Feasts of Life *Jim Vlaun*	$12.95
From Holy Hour to Happy Hour *Francis X. Gaeta*	$7.95
Grace Notes *Lorraine Murray*	$9.95
Healing through the Mass *Robert DeGrandis, SSJ*	$9.95
Our Grounds for Hope *Fulton J. Sheen*	$7.95
The Healing Rosary *Mike D.*	$5.95
Healing Your Grief *Ruthann Williams, OP*	$7.95
Life, Love and Laughter *Jim Vlaun*	$7.95
Living Each Day by the Power of Faith *Barbara Ryan*	$8.95
Loving Yourself for God's Sake *Adolfo Quezada*	$5.95
The Joy of Being an Altar Server *Joseph Champlin*	$5.95
The Joy of Being a Catechist *Gloria Durka*	$4.95
The Joy of Being a Eucharistic Minister *Mitch Finley*	$5.95
The Joy of Being a Lector *Mitch Finley*	$5.95
The Joy of Being an Usher *Gretchen Hailer, RSHM*	$5.95
The Joy of Marriage Preparation *McDonough/Marinelli*	$5.95
The Joy of Music Ministry *J.M. Talbot*	$6.95
The Joy of Preaching *Rod Damico*	$6.95
The Joy of Teaching *Joanmarie Smith*	$5.95
The Joy of Worshiping Together *Rod Damico*	$5.95
Lights in the Darkness *Ave Clark, O.P.*	$8.95
Meditations for Survivors of Suicide *Joni Woelfel*	$8.95
Mother Teresa *Eugene Palumbo, S.D.B.*	$5.95
Personally Speaking *Jim Lisante*	$8.95
Practicing the Prayer of Presence *Muto/van Kaam*	$8.95
Prayers from a Seasoned Heart *Joanne Decker*	$8.95
Praying the Lord's Prayer with Mary *Muto/van Kaam*	$8.95
Praying through Our Lifetraps *John Cecero, SJ*	$9.95
Rising from the Ashes *Adolfo Quezada*	$4.95
5-Minute Miracles *Linda Schubert*	$4.95
Season of New Beginnings *Mitch Finley*	$4.95
Season of Promises *Mitch Finley*	$4.95
St. Katharine Drexel *Daniel McSheffery*	$12.95
Stay with Us *John Mullin, SJ*	$3.95
Surprising Mary *Mitch Finley*	$7.95
What He Did for Love *Francis X. Gaeta*	$5.95
Woman Soul *Pat Duffy, OP*	$7.95
You Are My Beloved *Mitch Finley*	$10.95

For a free catalog call 1-800-892-6657
Visit our website: www.catholicbookpublishing.com